PRAISE FOR

Screenwriting Fundamentals

"A number of excellent references are available on screenplay writing. Don Simonds has immersed himself in these and extracted their essences in his highly useful guide, *Screenwriting Fundamentals*. His textbook, taken from his college-level Introduction to Screenwriting course, is clear and thorough. It not only gives a screenwriter the needed tools for developing a screenplay, it also provides motivation, leaving the reader with an "I can do that" feeling. Don references a wide variety of sources ranging from Aristotle to McKee and presents them in an easily digestible format. I studied screenplay writing when I learned how structurally similar it is to novels, and I believe novelists and playwrights will find many sections applicable to their art. The chapters on scene creation and character development are the equal of any guide to creative writing. When I sat down to review Don's book, I found myself putting pen to paper for a screenplay I'd had gestating in the back of my mind. Find your inspiration wherever you can, but for now I can recommend *Screenwriting Fundamentals* as a cutting-edge tool for the creative writers of all venues."

- William Dean Patterson Award-winning author
Deathgod
Member, The Dramatists Guild

"Veteran academic Don Simonds, after years of laboring in the trenches inspiring young writers to strut their stuff, has gathered his wealth of knowledge into a very painstakingly researched, incredibly detailed book: *Screenwriting Fundamentals*.

Although designed as a text/teaching tool, the volume offers much more. Built around the always solid 30/60/30-page distribution system, the vital areas of character arc, imagery, titles, and other necessities build toward a very well-written Tranby Croft screenplay which offers, by example, a basic connect-the-dots method of screenplay creation. He succinctly includes often forgotten areas: marketing, guard your thoughts and screenplays carefully, and the finer points of introductory correspondence, to list a few. The effect is excellent, particularly for the newcomer in the art."

- Gary Clifton Author
Burn Sugar Burn
www.bareknucklethoughts.org

"This is the most comprehensive and concise book I've seen on the subject. What sets it apart from others? The examples, hands-on practice at the end of each chapter and the detailed explanations. This is a book that any writer can benefit from, whether writing a screen treatment, screenplay or novel. (By the way, I loved the way you broke down the differences between the three.) The principles apply to any well-told story. It is a book I will keep in my reference library and refer to often. It's a great way to stay on track, focused and moving forward in the right direction."

- **Jan Sikes** Award-winning author
www.jansikes.com

"*Screenwriting Fundamentals* is a concise, interesting study into the writing of a screenplay. The book takes one through the intricacies of the screenwriting process. I particularly enjoyed reading Scene 8 - Strategies for Rewriting and Sequence Three - Final Draft. Sequence Four provides ideas for getting your play sold.

Screenwriting Fundamentals is a fantastic resource in learning all the facets of screenwriting from start to finish."

- **Barry Limoges, Ph.D.** Author
Private McCormick's Escape

also by Donald E. Simonds

Achieving on Purpose:
Your GUIDE to Managerial Success

Bandits of Time:
The Laws for Improving Personal Effectiveness

Screenwriting Fundamentals

by

Donald E. Simonds, M.Ed.

ISBN-13: 978-1717042514
ISBN-10: 1717042511

Cover design by Donald E. Simonds
Author photograph by Simonds Photography

DEDICATION

To my student congregation which has become more successful as a result of practicing these techniques, and to the future of the craft via readers of this book.

ACKNOWLEDGEMENTS

When I completed my junior year at the University of Tennessee, I transferred to Florida State University to finish my undergraduate degree. I was required to take some freshman courses due to curriculum differences. My favorite course was called, An Introduction to Theatre and the text book was, *The Season, A Candid Look at Broadway* by William Goldman. Had I taken it as a freshman, I would have majored in drama. To the FSU Théâtre Department, especially Chuck Metcalf, for inspiring me to continue my studies after graduation.

To Sam Havens, Professor Emeritus at the University of St. Thomas in Houston for teaching me dramatic writing. I studied playwriting and penned my first stage play under his tutelage.

Furthermore, I enrolled in the film program at UCLA Extension where professors were industry professionals. To all the excellent instructors, especially the late Don Richardson, for furthering my understanding of Motion Picture Arts and Sciences.

During my Master's curriculum at the University of Texas, I minored in Radio, Film, Television where I completed a feature film script and produced an industrial video that I still use in my course called, Innovation Process Management. To those professors for the practical experience.

Finally, my personal library is filled with more than 100 books on creative writing, particularly cinematic technique. To the authors of the books on screenwriting that I have consumed which have helped me understand the craft.

I thank all those who've helped me along my journey.

D. E. S.

Plano, TX
January 10, 2018
www.theentertrainerpro.com

CONTENTS

Sequence One
Pre-Production

Scene 1

Getting Started

The "go" decision is the ultimate importance of the studio executive. They are responsible for what gets up there on the silver screen. Compounding their problem of no job security in the decision-making process is the single most important fact, perhaps, of the entire movie industry:

NOBODY KNOWS ANYTHING

– William Goldman, *Adventures in the Screen Trade*

In other words, you cannot second-guess what some studio executive will buy or green light; so, write what *you think* will make an exceptional film.

What is a Screenplay?

The dictionary defines screenplay like this:

n. – a *story* written in a *form* suitable for production as a movie.

How do you know your story is not a song, stage play, or novel? Where is your passion? Which do you want to write; a song, stage play, novel or movie? They all have a beginning, middle, and end (plot) that makes a point. So, the difference must be in *form,* or general structure.

A song is a story written in the *form* of poetry and set to music with the intent of being heard by the audience. It is usually short and conveys one clear thought.

A stage play is a story written in the *form* of conversation and enacted live in the presence of an audience.

A novel is a story written in the *form* of thoughts and feelings with the intent of being read by the audience.

A screenplay is a story written in the *form* of pictures revealing action and external events which are to be seen by the audience.

Notice the differences in the following samples of form:

In his jail cell, Tony paces as Big Al walks up.

Tony

I'm up for parole, man. Now what?

Big Al

What'd ya mean? You're getting outta this hell hole.

Tony

What's waiting for me at home?

Big Al

That gal of yours.

Tony

How can I be sure?

Big Al

Write her a letter … tell her you're comin' home.
She'll be there.

Tony

What if she doesn't want an ex-con, man?

Big Al

Tell her to leave you a sign, man. If it's not there,
you keep on truckin', dig?

Tony

Yeah, okay. It'll be my fault for messin' up our lives.

Big Al

Right … She'll be there … if she loves you, man.

<u>**A Novel**</u>

Tony paced like a caged lion around his prison cell in Huntsville, Texas. He had just received word his parole was granted. What to do? His mind reeled. He was going home but all he could think about was Carla. Carla had been his high school sweetheart, with the emphasis on sweet. Then he'd fouled up. He'd gotten in with the wrong crowd. In fact, he'd just been driving the car but hadn't committed any of the vandalism or thefts. Nevertheless, he was the "wheel man," as the prosecutor had emphasized repeatedly. That bastard just wanted to get another notch on his belt.

He stared at a picture of Carla in his cell. He'd admired that picture every day for the last three years, the longest years of his life. And now, on the day he learned he'd be paroled, he was more scared than he'd been during the sentencing.

What if she's found someone else? If she doesn't want me, then what? Big Al had given him some good advice. "Write her a letter," Al had said. "Tell her you're coming home. Tell her to give you a sign." *That might work.*

Carla had the biggest brown eyes, like melted chocolate. And her lips, like cherries … *Hey, get a grip; you're supposed to be writing a letter. Tell her you love her. What should the sign be?*

If the sign isn't there I'll just keep on truckin'. A man takes responsibility for his actions. Right?

Tony wasn't religious but he bowed his head, "Please God, let her still want me."

<u>**A Screenplay**</u>

INT. HUNTSVILLE PRISON - TONY'S CELL - DAY

TONY, 26 years old, dark hair, dark eyes, stands 5'
11," 180 pounds, paces like a caged lion. Although
handsome by any standard, he currently looks like a man
in anguish. BIG AL, 6' 3," and 300 pounds looks like
his namesake from the Country Bear Jamboree. Al enters
the cell as quietly as a church mouse.

                         Big Al
               What's up?

Tony springs, out of his wits with fear, spins, and
lands like a ninja, hands up in defensive Kung Fu
position, ready to fight. He faces his predator, sees
it's Al, then drops his hands abruptly.

                         Tony
               Christ Almighty. You want to knock,
               Mother?

                         Big Al
               Whoa, Brother, I heard you were
               leaving this paradise.

                         Tony
               Yeah, I'm goin' home. To what? I
               don't know.

BIG AL

Big Al scratches his chin, then raises his eye brows.
He's got it.

                         Big Al
               Write Carla a letter; tell her to
               leave you a visual of some kind.

TONY

His expression changes as he contemplates the
possibilities.

                         Tony
               And if there's no sign, I keep on
               truckin'.

ANOTHER ANGLE

Big Al gives Tony a farewell bear hug.

What was the song, from which these samples were adapted?

To get the most from this book, it might be useful for you to think of a story you'd like to write. As you work your way through the text, practice by completing the Scene's purpose for your own story. Let's start with the genre you want to write. The following is a short list of the kinds of genres to which you might apply the skills in this book:

• Drama	• Comedy
• Mystery	• Romantic Comedy
• Suspense	• Black Comedy
• Thriller	• Farce
• Science Fiction	• Comedy of Manners
• Tragedy	• Theatre of the Absurd
• Western	• Action/Adventure

There are 140 genres listed on the internet. Most are a combination of genres created for marketing purposes. As a writer, it's important for you to maintain focus on a single genre. Don't try to write a "Mystery-Romance-Adventure." Pick one. The script I'll be using as my primary example is suspense. It has a romantic sub-plot, but the story is clearly in the suspense genre. This will help you make creative choices.

The Premise

The dictionary defines premise like this:

n. – a previous statement serving as a basis for an *argument.*

Before writing the script, the writer must determine many things. After genre, what *argument* will be proven? The writer must have an idea that will ensure progress toward an objective according to plan. Each creative choice is guided by the premise.

The inspiration of your story may have come from playing the "what if" game. For instance, the inspiration for my murder story started like this, *"What if a sketch artist draws a likeness of a murderer and then the murderer threatens her?"*

By contrast, the premise is like a parable – a story that teaches a moral or life lesson – What is the lesson you want to teach?

The premise is expressed in a single sentence with three parts:

1.   The *virtue* or life value your main character learns or teaches
2.   The *vice* or dramatic antagonism
3.   The *result* or desirable consequences of the *moral*

The best stories have a premise which helps the audience believe the story is a truthful metaphor for life.

My original premise wasn't very well defined but I knew I wanted it to be about justice and my main character's creativity. So, I started with, "*Justice prevails because the ingenuity of the Protagonist is greater than that of the Antagonist.*"

In Lajos Egri's book, *The Art of Dramatic Writing* (originally published in 1942 under a different title), he provides examples of premises. Most are from playwrights such as Shakespeare, Moliere, Ibsen, Kingsley, and Tennessee Williams. What follows are some representative examples:

Optimistic writers usually tell inspiring stories which focus on Honesty, Loyalty, Generosity, etc. Some examples of optimistic premises might be:

- Charity triumphs when we sacrifice our needs for the unloved
- Honesty defeats deceitfulness
- Righteousness does not rejoice in wrongdoing

Pessimistic writers tell cynical stories focusing on vices like Dishonesty, Unfaithfulness, Gluttony, etc. Some examples of pessimistic premises might be:

- Foolish generosity leads to poverty
- Promiscuity leads to jealousy and murder
- Friendship is destroyed by heedlessness

Some writers write ironic stories with an up and down ending. The Protagonist achieves the goal but is destroyed by it or must give up something of equal or greater value.

Some examples of ironic premises might include:

- Love is both pleasure and pain pursued to give life meaning
- Fame isn't worth the price of freedom
- Ruthless ambition leads to its own destruction

Many authors and educators suggest that new writers should write what they know. Do you know what it's like to murder someone? How many writers of westerns, crime stories, murder mysteries, etc. have first-hand knowledge of their subject?

A better maxim is to "write what you believe." Write the truth from your point of view.

Do you believe "Great love defies even death?" If so, then write your version of Romeo and Juliette.

The Subject Matter

Once you have decided on the genre and premise, it's time to focus on answering questions about the subject matter. Here are the four most important decisions and an example of how I answered them for my story:

1. What is the logline? This is like a cable guide description or an extension of your answer to the "what if" game. For example:

A Crime Illustrator is propelled into a race for her life when she sketches an exact likeness of a murder suspect and becomes his object of pursuit.

A great way to find examples of loglines is to refer to my friend Doug King's book, *Loglines*. He also has a blog about loglines called *Loglines "R" Us* at https://loglinesrus.wordpress.com. You can also search the web for "Best Loglines" you'll find a plethora of examples. Finally, beware of the movie loglines on the cable guide of your cable provider. Most focus on the actors in the film rather than the description.

2. What is the time (period & duration) and place of the story?

My story takes place in San Francisco during the summer of 1984. The duration is July 4th through 18th.

3. Who tells the story? Options include: the writer (omniscient), a character narrator (Red from Shawshank Redemption), the Protagonist (first person), or the Antagonist (first person).

I, the writer, am telling this story.

4. Who are the characters? How many do you need? What are their purposes? My rule of thumb is to have no more than five primary characters. You'll need:

a Protagonist – someone the audience roots for,
an Antagonist – someone the audience roots against,
and up to three others, perhaps:
> *a comic relief,*
> *a buddy for the Protagonist,*
> *an accomplice for the Antagonist, or*
> *a love interest, etc.*

Supporting characters should be created based upon how they will interact with the central character, bringing out the central character's traits and behaviors that will eventually prove the premise. Here is how I started my list of characters:

Tranby Croft – Protagonist/central character
Martin Mayhew – Antagonist
Harris Richardson – love interest
Detective Mitchell Fields – police team leader
Melinda Gary – Bay-Tips news anchor

There may be other minor characters (i.e. Ross and McNally are part of the police team and will provide comic relief and Aaron is the Antagonist's sidekick). I'll also have limited roles for the victim's family members, the eyewitness, other cops etc.

Dramatic Structure

The paradigm for dramatic structure starts with the three-act play. Within this basic structure, there are seven elements that must be planned before the script writing can begin. These elements are:

1. The Balance
2. The Disturbance
3. The Plan
4. The Obstacles
5. The Crisis
6. The Climax
7. The Outcome or New Balance

I've used a 120-page model for these descriptions. A screenplay typed in the correct format with the correct font (**Courier or Courier New 12 pt.**) will play at one minute per page. So, 120 pages equals two hours. Today, many scripts are written at 110 pages. Use the same ratio regardless of script length. This means Act I is 25% of the script, Act II is 50%, and Act III is 25%.

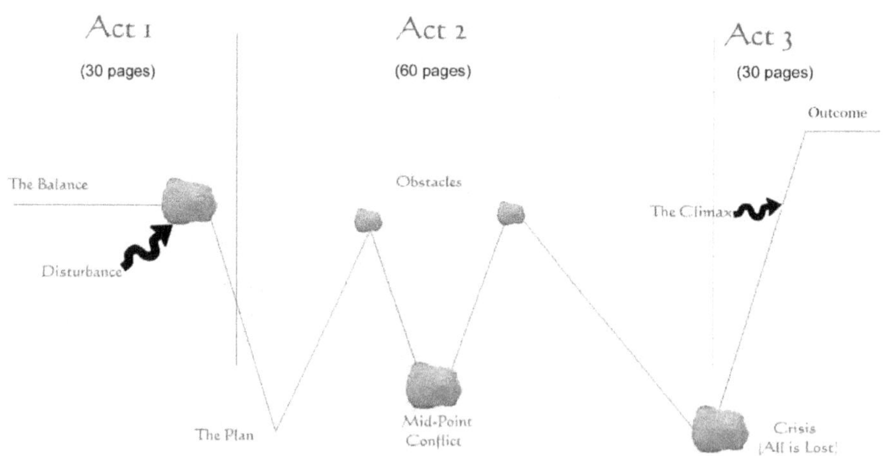

Let's look at what must be accomplished within each element.

The Balance (pages 1-24)

The first ten pages are the most important. They set the stage for the show. Viewers or readers need to know enough in the first ten minutes to decide if they like it or not. My first ten pages cover these things:

  Page 1 – The setting is San Francisco

  Page 2 – A murder takes place (dramatic incident to hook the viewers)

  Pages 3-6 – Detectives investigate

  Pages 7-10 – Central character is introduced

The Balance should explain the status quo. That means, what is happening in the central character's life at the time the show begins. Notice how I depicted it in the diagram as a flat line. The main character's life is just going along. Pages 10-24 can be used to introduce secondary characters, elude to the premise, create a mood, or introduce thematic devices.

The Disturbance (pages 25-30)

Approximately 25 pages (minutes) into the story something happens to change the status quo. The Disturbance is the plot point that drives the rest of the show.

There may be many twists and turns but the two most significant ones spin the story in another direction and require the central character to act or react to the situation. The first is the Disturbance. I call it the Disturbance, because it disturbs the status quo. It turns the main character's life topsy-turvy.

Quite often the Disturbance is the introduction of a new character, perhaps the Antagonist, and sets the stage for the Plan.

The Plan (pages 31-44)

Essentially, the Plan is the beginning of the Story. The Protagonist must decide what to do about the Disturbance. The Plan is the central character's intention regarding the Disturbance. Will he get revenge, go into denial, run away from the problem, what?

Although the Plan is always improbable, almost impossible, it must be believable. If the Plan is so improbable that the audience cannot suspend its disbelief; then, the show will be unsuccessful.

The Plan is the central character's motivation. The Protagonist will do anything to carry out the Plan. **Do Not** let things happen to the central character. By this I mean, don't have someone else act to save the Protagonist. Rather, have the central character make all the decisions and take logical actions to carry out the Plan.

The Obstacles (pages 45-85)

The complications keeping the Protagonist from accomplishing the Plan are the heart of the story. There is no drama without conflict.

Let me say it again. *There is no drama without conflict.*

Once we know what the Plan is (what the central character wants), we can create Obstacles to that goal. An old playwriting adage makes this analogous to putting the Protagonist up a tree (Disturbance) and throwing stones (Obstacles) at him. Although there is no magic number of stones to be thrown, start with three or four. Place them at fifteen-page intervals; 45, 60, and 75. Have the stones increase in magnitude until we reach the seemingly unsolvable problem.

The Crisis (pages 86-90)

The second and most important plot-point is called the Crisis, that unsolvable problem, the "all is lost" moment. This is usually a confrontation between two people, probably the Protagonist and the Antagonist. At this moment, the audience should be thinking, "Well that's it. The hero will not make it out of this one."

The Climax (pages 91-115)

The final direction needs to be a creative way to get the Protagonist out of that darn tree. As in the Balance, the writer must answer several questions:

> - How does it end?
> - What happens to the central character?
> - Does the Plan succeed or fail?
> - Was the Premise proved?

A strong ending resolves the story to the audience's satisfaction. It must be comprehensible; a moment of realization, complete.

The Outcome (pages 115-120)

The New Balance. Notice in the structure diagram, I drew the Outcome as a straight line again. Like the Balance, the Outcome is the new status quo, the new normal for the main character. It's different, but as it should be.

As an audience member, I want to leave the theatre knowing what happens next. At least, I want to be able to construct my own epilogue without seeing it.

Sometimes, like in Butch Cassidy and the Sundance Kid, the Protagonists die. So, the New Balance is "the world is safe from these two crooks" or "The Legend Begins." Give me enough to make up my own mind.

<u>**Your Turn**</u>

Complete the following exercises:
1.	Dissect *The Tranby Croft Affair* ("TCA") synopsis – find the seven plot elements of the story.
2.	Watch your favorite movie – find the seven plot elements and write a synopsis of the film. You might want to watch the movie twice. First, all the way through; then, scene by scene.
3.	Prepare or fine tune your Premise.
4.	Answer the subject matter questions for your story.
5.	Prepare a synopsis of your story including all seven plot elements. This can be from 1 – 4 pages, such as:

	Act I – Up to 1 ½ pages including the Balance and Disturbance.

	Act II – A paragraph or two describing each of the components; the Plan, three or four Obstacles, and the Crisis.

	Act III – Up to one page for the Climax and the Outcome.

SYNOPSIS

"The Tranby Croft Affair"
by
Donald E. Simonds

Crime Illustrator, Tranby Croft, works for the San Francisco Police Department and provides drawings for a segment called *Bay-Tips* on the local television station. *Bay-Tips* shows crime scene details or reenactments and offers rewards for information leading to arrests in hopes that citizens will call with information. The host of the show is a stereotypical news anchor named Melinda Gary.

Detective Mitchell Fields asks Tranby to draw a composite from an eye witness account and she creates an extraordinarily accurate likeness of the murderer. The picture airs during the six o'clock *Bay-Tips* show, during which Tranby's name is inadvertently mentioned. The murderer sees the report, calls and threatens Tranby.

Harris Richardson, a mystery writer, also sees the report and approaches Tranby with a proposal to work together on a novel based upon some of her exploits. She reluctantly accepts his offer.

More murders occur and *Bay-Tips* airs the picture of the suspect again. The suspect begins stalking Tranby.

Romantic sparks fly between Harris and Tranby and, in his misguided zeal, Harris tries to protect Tranby by insisting she go into hiding. The police begin to suspect Harris is the murderer and Mitchell Fields advises Tranby to stay away from Harris. But alas, she follows her heart.

Meanwhile, Mitchell and his team's investigators uncover prime suspect Martin Mayhew.

Harris and Tranby consummate their relationship. Later that night, Harris spots Martin, recognizes him from Tranby's drawing, and chases him through Nob Hill, but Martin eludes Harris. A confrontation between Harris and Detective Fields leads to Harris' arrest for obstruction of justice.

Tranby becomes suspicious of Melinda Gary's use of her name on the air and devises a plan to trick her into disclosing what she knows about the perpetrator.

When Harris is released from jail, Martin follows him to Tranby's hiding place. Consequently, Martin and his sidekick get to Tranby but detective Fields arrives and he, Harris, and Tranby prevail.

Tranby goes back to work, Harris publishes his novel, entitled appropriately, "The Tranby Croft Affair," and they consider future collaborations.

Scene 2

Characters, Getting to Know Yours

The best index to a person's character is (a) how he treats people who can't do him any good, and (b) how he treats people who can't fight back.

– Abigail Van Buren

Character Design

Focusing on the people in a story is essential. It is essential to the plot. It is essential for intrigue. Without interesting people, your story will be boring.

What is Character? Let's call Webster's definitions the six elements of character:

1. A distinctive trait
2. Behavior typical of a person
3. Moral strength
4. Reputation
5. Status; position
6. An eccentric person

Now, look at these in the context of playwriting.

A distinctive trait	Does this character have any physical or emotional scars? A disfigured face would be a physical trait while a shy demeanor might be the visible sign of a deeply rooted emotional scar.
Behavior typical of a person	Two things are important here. First, behavior refers to one's conduct or how one acts (get it?). Second, typical indicates predictability…but in a story, we don't want the audience to predict what is going to happen…the audience needs consistency. This character needs to act in a

	believable way. Always remember, "Past behavior predicts future behavior."
Moral strength	What are the values that this person holds dear? How will the person react to a challenge of those beliefs? For the element of Moral Strength, ask, "What would this character's position be on today's (time period of the story) moral questions?" For instance, if writing in present day, you might ask your character to take a stand on these issues:

- Pro Choice or Pro Life
- Gun Control
- Political Correctness
- Smokers' Rights
- Censor Music, TV, or Movies
- Gay Marriage

What will this character fight for? Does this character feel strongly enough about any of these issues to stand in a picket line, write her Congressman, or become an advocate?

Reputation	What do other people believe about this character?
Status; position	This character could be the Mayor, a prominent figure, or he could be the Big Cheese within a clique.
An eccentric person	Any unconventional attributes might be considered eccentric.

These elements of character come from living and these six are a good place to start. If you want to dig deeper into your character, then exploring other components of human dynamics might help you. Things like Value Programing, the Johari Window, Zodiac signs, and Myers-Brigs Type Indicator (MBTI) can be useful in developing a character.

What follows is a closer look at these four options for developing character traits. Use the ones that make the most sense to you.

Value Programming

From the field of sociology, Morris Massey became a well-known scholar based upon his work, *What You Are Is Where You Were When.* "When" means when you were about 10 years old. Dr. Massey says each of us starts value programming when, at about 10, we start evaluating the world and how we relate to it.

For instance, a person who was 10 in 1929 will undoubtedly have been affected by the Great Depression. As an adult character in your story, this character value might be revealed by her stuffing cash into a mattress.

A 10-year-old Jew in 1944 Germany is going to need therapy for a long time. As your adult character, you might want to write a scene or two for him in a Psychiatrist's office to reveal the childhood trauma.

Did your character's parents get divorced when she was 10? This event is going to impact how she relates to men, marriage, and other aspects of her adult life.

Was your character's hero at the age of 10, Barry Bonds? As your adult character, you might write a scene or two showing him cheating to succeed in his profession.

So, the author must know from birth onward, what has happened to this character up to the point that the story begins. Otherwise, she won't know how this character will react to the stones that are thrown. In Syd Field's book, *Screenplay,* he calls this the Interior or Character Biography. What happens from the start of the movie he calls the Exterior. During the story, the writer will reveal the character's desires and typical behavior to satisfy those desires.

Consequently, as writers, we should know more about the character than the character knows about himself. This leads to a brief look through the Johari Window.

The Johari Window

In behavioral science, the Johari Window is used as a tool for understanding the development of trust. Simply stated, this model looks like a window with four panes. Each pane contains information about an individual. The size of each pane is determined by how much each person knows, which in turn is related to how willing and able each person is to share information and listen to others share.

	Known to the Main Character	Unknown to the Main Character
Known to Other Characters	**Open**	**Blind Spot**
Unknown to Other Characters	**Hidden Facade**	**Unknown Area**

Using the model becomes a matter of stacking information into each of the panes based upon this character's biography.

For example, a distinctive trait such as a disfigured face would be placed in the **Open** windowpane because it's visible to everyone. However, if the scar is on a person's inner thigh or is an emotional scar, it would be placed in the **Hidden Facade**.

If your character has allergies and snorts often, he is obviously aware of the allergies. He may be unaware of the impact all that snorting in public has on his co-workers. This is an example of something in the **Blind Spot**.

Finally, the **Unknown Area** contains information regarding things that have never happened to this person or that are repressed. The character has never had a gun pointed to her head by a bank robber; so, she doesn't know what she will do nor does anyone else (although viewers might argue that they could guess based upon other confrontations, no one knows for sure). Another character's self-image may be that he is not particularly creative, but he has repressed memory of a painting done as a child that won a blue ribbon. Technically, someone knows about this but for purposes of storytelling, the author might reveal this to the character at the same time that the audience finds out. Hence, the **Unknown** information moves into the **Open** quadrant on screen.

Creating **stacks** is one way of getting to know characters. A starting place is the Six Elements of Character. Try to write at least one bit of information for each element and place it in the Johari Window for this person. Then as ideas come to you, add them to the appropriate windowpane.

You may want to use 3x5 cards for each idea or just create a large window on 8.5 X 11 paper. The advantage to cards is that you can move them around without rewriting.

Zodiac Sign

A Writer's Digest article suggested using Linda Goodman's book, *Sun Signs* to identify character traits. Many people think that astrology is hogwash. Nevertheless, this book is a wealth of characterization. I recommend assigning a birthday to each of your main characters, whether you are a believer or not. Here is an excerpt to ponder:

Perhaps the best way to get you to appreciate your LIBRA woman is to give you a quick run-down on what you would face with other sun signs in a simple situation. Let's say you are discussing the subject of calling cards. Should people use them today? Are they old fashioned? And what should they look like? Take a fast flight around the zodiac. Pretend that you are the only man in the room with twelve women. (That should be a pleasant supposition) The discussion should run something like this:

Aries:	Don't need them, I use the telephone.
Taurus:	It's rare that I go calling. People visit me.
Gemini:	Calling cards! Who has time for calling cards?
Leo:	Well, if they were really wild and impressive looking---
Virgo:	I'll have to check Emily Post and see exactly what she says.
Sagittarius:	My gawd! You mean people still take time for that junk?
Scorpio:	If they're not home, they miss me. It's their loss, not mine.
Aquarius:	I wonder if it's raining outside? I thought I heard thunder.
Cancer:	Cards are so impersonal. I'd rather write a note.
Pisces:	I always sense when people aren't there, and I only call on them when I get a subliminal message they want to see me.
Capricorn:	The custom is perfectly proper. But there's no point in discussing the design. If it's not engraved, it's not a calling card.
Libra:	Well, it all depends. If you want to do the correct thing, you should have them. It's a

charming gesture. On the other hand, using them might seem pretentious today, and the modern woman is too busy to bother with them. Of course, you have to consider the reason behind the custom. Then again, there are people who can't afford calling cards. If it is a strain on the budget, then they aren't really necessary. Looking at the other side of it, however, I can't help feeling the beauty and grace of yesterday is missing in today's frantic pace, so it might…

So, you get the point that each person has a different personality. At least twelve of them exist for males and twelve for females.

Myers-Briggs Type Indicator

One last point regarding how a writer can build character traits. Consider assigning MBTI to each character. In behavioral science, the MBTI is used to help people understand their temperament which identifies an individual's attitudes and actions. Isabel Myers and Kathryn Briggs developed a questionnaire to identify different types of personality inspired by Carl Jung's book *Psychological Types*. The questionnaire identifies basic preferences of four dichotomies; 1) Favorite world, 2) Information, 3) Decisions, and 4) Structure, which are drawn from Jung's theory. What's your preference?

Favorite World	Do you prefer to focus on the outer world or your own inner world?
	Extroversion (E) ———— Introversion (I)
Information:	Do you prefer to focus on the basic information you take in or do you prefer to interpret and add meaning?
	Sensing (S) ———— Intuition (N)
Decisions:	When making decisions, do you prefer to first look at logic and consistency or first look at people and special circumstances?
	Thinking (T) ———— Feeling (F)
Structure:	In dealing with the outside world, do you prefer to get things decided or do you prefer to stay open to new information and options?
	Judging (J) ———— Perceiving (P)

Each of these dichotomies is shown as a continuum which means when each person is assessed, the result could be one of the extremes or someplace in the middle. For instance: I am an extreme introvert; so, I find it difficult to introduce myself in an unfamiliar setting. And since I focus on the inner world, I can easily tune the noise out and literally get lost in my thoughts. On the second continuum, I am right in the middle. I believe I was born an (S) and moved just right of center as I became an adult. Therefore, the way I lean is dependent upon the situation. If I were on a jury, I would want the factual information. If I were decorating my home, I'd want to interpret the data as it pertained to my life style. On the last two I'm roughly at the 25% mark from the left, a strong (T) and (J) but not extreme.

There are 16 combinations of these four. Each profile has strengths and weaknesses. As a INTJ, I have high self-confidence, am motivated by independence, stay open-minded, and feel capable of doing anything I set my mind to do. On the other hand, others might see my confidence as arrogance, my rational arguments as judgmental, my analytical prowess as neurotic perfectionism, and my disdain for highly structured environments as an aversion to being a team player.

Once you have assigned a MBTI to your main character then you can start to flush out the character traits that will be disclosed during the story.

To learn more about MBTI, simply do an internet search using "MBTI." You should see the following two links pop up on the first page:

http://www.myersbriggs.org/my-mbti-personality-type/mbti-basics/

https://www.16personalities.com/free-personality-test

Furthermore, I highly recommend *Please Understand Me II,* by David Keirsey in which he breaks down the temperament, character, and personality of the 16 types.

Finally, remember there is no drama without conflict. I was recently referred to a blog about how each MBTI type reacts to stress. You should book mark this page. It is a wealth of information regarding stressors and stress-busting techniques:

http://psychologyjunkie.com/2015/08/02/how-each-mbti-type-reacts-to-stress-and-how-to-help/

In summary, there are several ways to approach characterization. Each writer must decide which techniques are the most productive. Syd Field calls it creative research. The main objective at this stage of preparation is to get to know the characters so well, that it's obvious what the character will do or say when the writing begins. The only way to be that prepared is to complete the research and summarize it in the form of a character biography.

Cast Design

In Robert McKee's book, *Story,* he states, "In essence, the Protagonist creates the rest of the cast. All other characters are in the story first and foremost because of the relationship they strike to the Protagonist and the way each helps to delineate the dimensions of the Protagonist's complex nature."

In other words, if Tranby Croft is going to demonstrate courage, another character must incite that response. Also, since we are all combinations of opposites (I can be a nice guy or I can be a mean snake), another character must provoke the cowardice in her.

Starting with the eight traits I thought were most critical to the story and most want to display in Tranby, I created the following table:

Fields	Harris	Tranby	Martin	Melinda
	Adventurous	Courageous		
	Sensual	Flirtatious		
		Determined		Devious
		Cautious		Scheming
		Standoffish	Controlling	
		Cowardly	Evil	
Protective		Careless		
Teacher		Indecisive		

You can see, by proximity of the traits, Martin's evilness will bring out Tranby's cowardice. When Harris is adventurous, Tranby will react courageously. When Tranby is indecisive, Mitchell will be her teacher.

Feel free to add secondary characters, if you wish. For instance, I have Ross as Comic Relief from Mitchell's Intensity and McNally behaving Ineptly when Mitchell threatens his subordinates.

Character Names

A note about Character names. It's a common habit to create characters beginning with the same letter of the alphabet. Novices and pros alike fall into this pattern which can become confusing for the reader. In my draft of TCA, can you identify my favorite letter?

In my Script Consultant role, being cognizant of this habit, it has become one of my top five feedback points to my clients. For instance, one manuscript had seven characters whose names started with the letter "C.", six characters with the letter "S", and three of those "S" names were identical. Yes, three different characters named Sam.

Be cognizant of the letters you choose for your characters' names. Don't use the same letter for more than one character. I love the film, *A Few Good Men* but which one's Dawson and which one's Downey? The exception *may* be in naming twins or referencing historical figures. For example, Charlie Chaplin instructs Winston Churchill on the subtleties of being a tramp, would be acceptable.

Here is a simple task to eliminate this habit. At the top of a piece of paper write, "Cast of Characters." Down the left-hand side write the alphabet. Place your main characters on first and eliminate those letters. Never use the same letter twice.

Your Turn

Complete the following exercises:
1. Watch your favorite movie again. This time look for character traits in scenes.
2. Decide who your Protagonist is and who your Antagonist is.
3. Write character biographies for each of them.
4. Decide which and how many other characters will be needed.
5. Start character bios for them as well.
6. Create a Cast Design table for your main characters.

CHARACTER BIOGRAPHY
OF
TRANBY CROFT

Tranby Katherine Croft was born September 25, 1956 in Washoe Hospital, Reno, Nevada. Her parents loved the name Katherine, but were concerned that Kathy Croft was too cutesy and the children might tease her; so, they decided to use it as the middle name. There have been many family debates over the years as to the origin of the name Tranby, which usually ended in arguments that Tranby had to stop by saying, "Hey, it really doesn't matter. I was just curious."

Tranby was a lovely child. "Cute as a button," her dad would say. She had dark brown hair from birth, which she wore in a Dorothy Hamill style before Dorothy Hamill knew what a Dorothy Hamill style was. She has the most beautiful translucent teal eyes, her most distinctive feature. She could mesmerize the coolest, hippest boys in school with those eyes. In junior high school, the self-proclaimed "stud on campus" looked into those dreamy green eyes, became weak in the knees, and fell to the ground.

If there was anything Tranby hated as a child, it was making a choice. But, if a choice was to be made, you'd better not rush her. And, above all, don't yell, shout, or holler because that hurt her eardrums and disturbed her equilibrium.

Luckily, Mrs. Croft was sensitive to her Libra child's delicate sense of balance; so, Tranby grew up with no significant neurosis about choices. And, that Libra caution was instrumental in keeping her out of trouble.

She had the happiest of childhoods. Tranby played well with others and made friends easily, but was selective with the ones she let into her inner circle. This could be because she was an only child.

Tranby was a great student. She did better in math than history and loved all forms of artistic expression. She loved it when her mother took her to her first play and she got to meet the actor in the cat costume. She played several musical instruments and was in the marching band in junior high school. But, art was Tranby's first love and always would be. She admired the paintings of the Masters at a very early age. By high school, she knew Art would be her college major.

She modeled clothing for a local department store during her senior year in high school and worked in the junior's department selling clothes to earn money for college.

In the fall of 1974, Tranby entered San Francisco State University as an Art major. She lost her virginity that fall to a boy named Rick Swagman, who eventually asked her to marry him, but she opted to finish her degree program and start her career. She loved Rick deeply and would have considered marriage had she been ten years older.

As she moved from childhood into the adult phase of her life, her basic values became validated through the college experience. She became an advocate for the pro-choice movement on campus. In fact, at a rally she once commented, "Pro-lifers don't really get it." In her infinite Libra wisdom, she decided the Constitution gave Americans freedom of choice. Pro-lifers wanted to take that choice away and remove that freedom.

Now, if she became pregnant, she would choose life; but don't even think about taking her right to choose away. Them's fight'n words. Similarly, she is against gun control or control of any kind, especially if it's the government doing the controlling.

Even smokers have rights. They may be making the wrong choice, but she would defend to the death their right to make the choice. Censor music, TV, or movies? How prudish!

Tranby is the quintessential feminine creature but she is not weak or helpless. This womanly creature is nine parts steel. She looks very cute in slacks and can be as masculine as needed, but she can be found in frilly organdy at parties and slinky silk in private. One of her most valuable assets is her ability to hide her sharp, keen mind behind utter femininity.

She graduated in the spring of 1978, right on schedule. Being on time is her only obsessive/compulsive behavior. She attributes this flaw to dear old Dad, who would rather sit for 30 minutes waiting at the train station than be 30 seconds late and watch the train pull away without him. He never preached this to her, she just watched her role model and that's what he did.

Her first job was in the layout department of the San Francisco Chronicle, which she basically hated, but it paid the bills. She always felt a degree was unnecessary for the grunt work the newspaper had her doing. A year and a half later, while pasting up copy for the classifieds, she noticed an ad from the SFPD for a Crime Illustrator. She'd found her dream job. She put the ad in her purse instead of the paper; and took her portfolio to the HR department at City Hall.

On January 10, 1980, she began her career creating courtroom illustrations and working for BAY-TIPS a unique program directed to the community in an effort to find criminals at large. She loved the crime reenactment illustrations, which were shown on television with the hope of jogging someone's memory of something they witnessed that might provide a clue or assist law enforcement in locating a suspect.

Her first assignment involved the murder of a 17-year-old high school athlete. He'd been abducted from his part-time job at a drive-in dairy and was found two days later in the desert, shot in the back. Tranby recreated a scene in which the boy was wearing his letterman's jacket and running with his arms up and arching his back when the bullet struck him. It worked. The day after it aired, SFPD got several calls that led to an arrest and she was hooked.

It is now 1984, as our story begins. At the age of 28, Tranby lives alone in an apartment on Sacramento Street near the corner of Polk Street. No one will ever know how unhappy she is living alone. Every day she dreams of her prince charming and wonders when she will find Mr. Right. Luckily, she works with a variety of people on the police force and at the television station. Otherwise, her work would also be alone and that would be too much to endure.

You may want to use a form like this for your minor characters:

CHARACTER BIOGRAPHY
OF

____

Character's role: ____

Date & place of birth: ____

Distinctive traits: ____

____

____

Typical behavior: ____

____

Moral strength: ____

____

Reputation: ____

____

Status; position: ____

____

Eccentric traits: ____

As the story begins:

Age: ____

Goals: ____

____

____

Needs: ____

____

____

Emotions: ____

____

Scene 3

Scene Outlining

To every action there is an equal and opposite reaction.

– Sir Isaac Newton *Philosophiæ Naturalis Principia Mathematica*

How to Start the Scene Outlining Process

Screenplays are composed of acts, sequences, scenes and beats (more on beats in Scenes 4 and 8). Acts are the largest component. Acts were discussed in Scene 1 and you were to have written a synopsis of your story covering the seven plot elements. You'll want to have that handy as you begin outlining.

Sequences are a series of scenes that accomplish one purpose. For example, I have a sequence of three scenes to introduce the love sub-plot. The first scene is when Harris lays eyes on Tranby for the first time. In the next scene, he accompanies her to the television studio. In the third scene, he escorts her back to her apartment. This represents the "Boy meets Girl" sequence.

The scene is the most basic unit of dramatic action. It consists of a camera placement, a location, and a time. If any of these elements change, the scene changes. If the camera is placed inside a home (INT.) and then is placed out on the lawn (EXT.), the scene has changed from inside to outside. If the location changes from the lawn to a football stadium, the scene has changed. If the time changes from Day to Night, the scene changes.

Scene Breakdown

One of the things I do for fun is breakdown movies into scenes. I start the DVD and watch the movie until the scene changes. Then I stop the DVD and write down a short sentence or phrase to describe the purpose of the scene. It might look like this for *Shakespeare in Love*:

Scene 1 – Henslowe's boots are on fire

Scene 2 – Introduce Will, his room

Scene 3 – Will and Henslowe discuss progress on the play, pay, etc.

Scene 4 – Will tells Dr. Moth of his Writer's Block

Scene 5 – Chamberlain's men perform at Whitehall Palace

Scene 6 – Introduce Queen, Viola (love interest), and Wessex (villain)

The purpose of this exercise is help you learn the flow of scenes, when the plot points occur, when sub-plots occur, the structure, and character devices used in excellent films. Before I start a new script of my own, I choose three to five films I have enjoyed and represent the genre I'm planning to write. I look for patterns among the scene outlines and then I write a scene breakdown for my story.

The duration of each scene in a movie ranges from 30 seconds to 5 minutes. There is no magic number but let's start with an average of 2-3 minutes per scene. There will be between 40 and 60 scenes. The original outline for TCA had 48 scenes and the script was 109 pages long. Average scene length is 2.4 minutes. Here is the original scene breakdown:

Scene Breakdown
For
The Tranby Croft Affair

1. Establishing shot – San Francisco
2. Introduce Tranby Croft
3. The TV Studio
4. Eyewitness comes forward
5. Composite drawing
6. Introduce Martin – kills a Chinese restaurant owner
7. Forensic scene – after the murder
8. Tranby's portrait of Martin appears on TV News
9. Introduce Harris Richardson – writer sub-plot
10. Harris and Tranby meet
11. Martin calls Tranby and threatens her
12. Harris finds out about the threat
13. Mitchell is investigating another murder
14. Martin's picture appears again on TV
15. Martin goes to Tranby's apartment
16. Tranby with Harris finds another threat on her bathroom mirror
17. Mitchell brings a forensic team to her apartment
18. Mitchell orders Detective Carter to tail Harris
19. Harris buys a gun, Carter reports
20. Harris starts working on the novel
21. Harris pleads with Tranby to hide
22. Harris enlists Susan (his sister) to help (bar/restaurant scene)
23. Harris & Susan take Tranby to a hideout/ have to lose Carter

24.   Martin goes to Tranby's – too many Cops – chase scene
25.   Harris is arrested for kidnapping Tranby
26.   Tranby is moved to another location
27.   Martin follows Harris when he is released from jail
28.   Mitchell follows to first hideout
29.   Shots of Carmel
30.   Tranby is taken on a tour of the gallery by Dennis
31.   Tranby and Harris act as if they are free
32.   The romantic interest comes to a consummation
33.   Martin puts out feelers to locate Tranby
34.   Susan lectures Harris for getting too close to real crime
35.   Tranby and Harris have a confrontation in Carmel
36.   Susan tells Tranby she has to be moved to Beverly Hills
37.   Next morning Martin and Aaron show up
38.   A chase starts when Martin finds the gallery
39.   Tranby leads Aaron into the Framing room
40.   Tranby kills Aaron with an artist's tool introduced in the Opening
41.   Martin grabs Susan as a hostage
42.   Melinda tells Mitchell the truth
43.   Tranby shoots Martin with Aaron's gun
44.   Mitchell arrives to shoot Martin again
45.   Harris says he has enough material for his book
46.   They all return to San Francisco
47.   Tranby goes back to work
48.   Harris shows Tranby the published book and asks if she will work with him again

Once you have the scene descriptors, it's time to do a storyboard of the scenes and thread them together in a coherent way. Using 3x5 cards for outlining allows for flexibility and experimentation in sequencing the scenes. It's like building a storyboard. You'll want to keep notes brief, but include:

1.   A heading (slug line)
2.   Who drives the scene
3.   The basic action
4.   What motivation and emotion will be played
5.   How the scene turns
6.   The conflict

A Heading (slug line) includes three parts

Camera Location	Scene Location	Time of Day
INT. or EXT.	SETTING	DAY or NIGHT

For Example:

- EXT. SAN FRANCISCO – DAY
- INT. COURTROOM – DAY
- INT. TRANBY'S APARTMENT – STUDIO – NIGHT

Who Drives the Scene?

Think about which character makes the decisions or which character's point of view is being explored. You don't have to explicitly write that on the card. It should be obvious by the way you write the action component. But it may help to make a note to remind yourself of the purpose of the scene to the story. Notice that I put a scene descriptor in my examples, like "Harris and Tranby Meet." This descriptor comes from my Scene Breakdown and it reminds me of what I hoped to accomplish in the scene.

The Basic Action

Describe the event with action verbs. Active voice refers to the arrangement of the sentence. Subject – Verb – Object. In active voice, the subject acts upon the object. In passive voice, the object comes first. This became crystal clear to me when a professor told me to do a global search of my manuscript for "is" and "are" and replace them with an action verb.

For instance, don't write, "The reports are pushed aside by Mitchell…." Rather, write, "Mitchell pushes the reports aside, reaches for the phone and dials the garage."

Furthermore, try to make the action verbs descriptive for the actor. Don't write, "Mitchell walks into the room." Instead, describe how he enters, "Mitchell struts into the room with the authority of a Wild West sheriff."

The action in a film script is always written in present tense. Therefore, do not use "was," "were," or "ed" suffixes as in "The reports were pushed…." Do use "Mitchell pushes the reports aside…."

Finally, think of each scene as a mini-story in which there is a Beginning, a Middle, and an End.

What Motivation and Emotion Will be Played?

At this stage of scene design, start to think like a Director. I studied Directing Actors for Stage and Screen at UCLA under Don Richardson, whose credits include more than 800 prime-time television shows. Two points made very clear by Mr. Richardson were, a Director must give the actor motivation and emotion to play. The scene must be actable.

In his book, *Acting without Agony,* Don Richardson writes, "For our purposes, *emotions are feelings large enough to change your life or destroy it.*" Hence, on the scene card put the feeling you want the character/actor to have when playing the scene. Such as, ambition, bliss, despair, ecstasy, blind rage, etc.

How the Scene Turns

McKee supports this idea of values/emotions and adds, "Ideally, every scene is a story event." To qualify as an event, the scene must cause the driving character to change emotions. In applying these last two points, the scene card might look like this:

Opening value (positive) – Tranby feels safe and secure
Ending value (negative) – She fears for her life

Every scene must turn from positive to negative or negative to positive. Otherwise, rewrite it or delete it from the script.

The Conflict

There is no drama without conflict. The conflict in the scene starts with whomever is driving the scene. That character wants something. Write the motivation in a simple sentence like, "To get the girl," "To gain her trust," "To win the job," etc. Then ask what blocks this desire and write it in an opposite way; such as, "To stop him from getting the girl," "To get away," "To hire someone else," etc. So, the scene card might look like this:

Conflict = He wants fresh ideas. She wants to be left alone.
He desires her. She rejects him.

When you are ready to complete the scene cards, review your Synopsis then write one scene card for each of the scenes in your breakdown. If you prefer, do scene cards from the Synopsis first. That is:

1. The Opening scene – page 1
2. The Disturbance – pages 25-30
3. The Plan – pages 31-44
4. The Obstacles – pages 45, 60, 75
5. The Crisis – pages 86-90
6. The Climax – pages 91-115
7. The Closing scene – pages 116-120

I'm a linear thinker; so, I prefer to write the cards in chronological order directly from the scene breakdown. Ultimately, you'll need cards for all the scenes before you begin writing the script, but create them in any order you wish.

You may include some occasional dialog but focus on the visual aspects of the scene. Here is a generic scene card example and then scenes 1, 10, and 11 from my breakdown as a guide:

```
Scene heading (slug line)
```

Scene Description	Purpose
Type description of scene and scene elements here	• Plot goal • Act goal • Core goal • Character goal • Sub-goal
	Characters • Protagonist • Antagonist • Supporting • Supporting

Link Action To:
Scenes where action builds to resolution in this scene, or whose action resolves issues from this screen.


```
EXT. SAN FRANCISCO - DAY
```

An establishing sequence of shots of the San Francisco Skyline	Purpose
– The Golden Gate Bridge – Alcatraz – Coit Tower – Cable Cars – Polk Street – Etc.	• To identify the setting • Romantic opening image
	Characters • None/Extras only

Link Action To:

EXT./INT. TRANBY'S STUDIO/APARTMENT - DAY

Harris and Tranby Meet

This scene begins outside Tranby's apartment. Harris rings her buzzer. She lets him in…He's obviously smitten…she finds out he is a writer and wants her to help him with an angle on a novel.

Opening value (negative) – Her indifference to him
Ending value (positive) – She's emotionally involved

Conflict = He wants fresh ideas. She wants to be left alone.

Purpose
- Boy meets girl sub-plot

Characters
- Protagonist – Tranby Croft
- Love interest – Harris Richardson

Link Action To:
Scene A of "Meet" sequence.

INT. TRANBY'S STUDIO/APARTMENT - NIGHT

Martin calls Tranby and threatens her

Tranby gets ready for bed. She takes off her clothes, brushes her teeth, slips under the covers. She breathes deeply, enters the second phase of sleep. The phone rings, it startles her. She groggily says hello. It's Martin (the murderer). He says, "…if I see my face on Channel 2 again, YOU'RE DEAD…."

Opening value (positive) – She feels safe and secure
Ending value (negative) – She fears for her safety

Conflict = Martin threatens Tranby's life.

Purpose
- The Disturbance
- Act I turning point

Characters
- Protagonist – Tranby Croft
- Antagonist – Martin Mayhew

Link Action To:
End of the Balance all scenes lead to this Plot point.

Your Turn

Complete the following exercises:

1.   Watch your favorite film again and do a scene breakdown.

2.   Do a scene breakdown for your story.

3.   Write the 40-60 scene cards for your story.

If you like the scene card format shown here, you may get the free PowerPoint by going to:

https://www.keepwriting.com/StorySorterTM.ppt

Scene 4

Screenplay Formatting

> Formatting is a key element of screenwriting, and is inseparable from it.
>
> – David Trottier *The Screenwriter's Bible*

Screenplay Stuff

When I was in college, I performed in the stage play *The Gingerbread Lady,* by Neil Simon. I played a Puerto Rican Grocery Clerk named Manuel, although in the script he was just called "Boy." The play was printed as a 5x7 booklet by Samuel French, Inc. and the script was formatted with the character name on the left margin then the dialog, like this:

Jimmy. Where were you? I thought you went out of business …

Boy. (At doorway) Mrs. Meara live here?

Jimmy. Yes Mrs. Meara lives here. … please put them in the kitchen.

Boy. (Not moving) Is fourteen dollars tweeny-eight cents.

Since this was the only script I had ever seen, I naturally thought it was a good model and I wrote my first screenplay like it. When my movie script was rejected, I asked the agent why. The first thing he said was that it wasn't formatted correctly and suggested that I get the book, *Teleplay,* by Coles Trapnell. I still have the book in my collection and much of what is in it remains relevant; however, there have been some changes in what Hollywood readers expect.

Keep in mind that you are writing a "spec script." Its purpose is to sell your story or your ability. Although screenwriting instructors may disagree on some of these points, one thing we all agree on is that you should not use camera and editing directions. The focus should be on narrative, the compelling visual action of the story. The "shooting script" will be written after your script is purchased.

There are several screenwriting software packages available today. I use Final Draft (which is the industry standard and what studios expect). Others include Movie Magic or Scrivener. If you're pressed for cash, you can get freeware at trelby.org, celtx.com, and storywriter.amazon.com. If you use screenwriting software, the formatting will be done for you. When writing your spec script disable Scene Numbering, Automatic Character Continueds, and Scene Breaks. Only include Slug Lines, Character Descriptions, Narrative, and Dialogue.

What follows are some guidelines on how to prepare the title page, page one, and subsequent pages. If you're not using screenwriting software, I'll include guidelines for margins and indents.

The Title Page

Position the title in all CAPS, in quotes, centered, approximately four inches from the top of the page. Then by and your name are in Upper and Lower case letters underneath the title.

Left justify your contact information at the bottom of the page starting approximately two to three inches from the bottom.

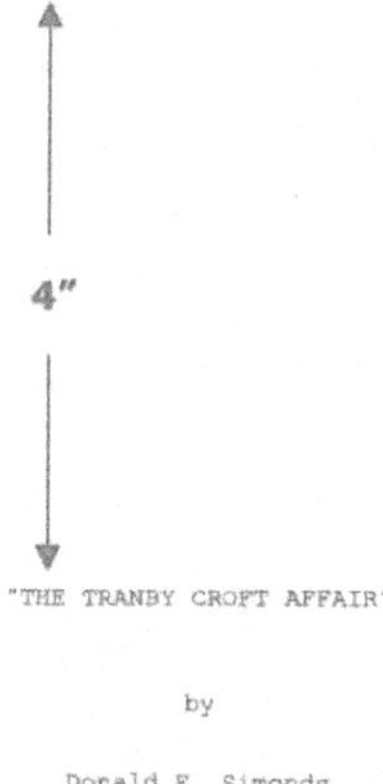

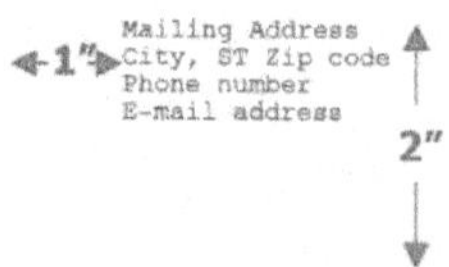

Page One

Place the title in all CAPS, in quotes, and centered on the top margin. Always, always, ALWAYS start the script with FADE IN in all CAPS followed by a colon. If you don't, the reader will assume you are an amateur and may throw your script in the slush pile.

```
FADE IN:
```

Follow FADE IN by a master scene heading in all CAPS. Notice this comes directly from your scene cards, such as:

```
EXT. SAN FRANCISCO - DAY
```

If you will have multiple sites within a location; such as, Tranby's Bedroom, Livingroom, Art Studio, etc. Go from the larger to the smaller location like this:

```
INT. TRANBY'S APARTMENT - BEDROOM - NIGHT
INT. TRANBY'S APARTMENT - ART STUDIO - DAY
INT. TRANBY'S APARTMENT - LIVINGROOM - NIGHT
```

Follow the master scene heading by narrative description (**4 lines max.**), such as:

```
Fog partially covers The Golden Gate Bridge. The
fog moves fast toward the San Francisco skyline.
```

If you need more than four lines to describe the action, break it into multiple paragraphs. Always write the narrative in present tense. You'll see I did that on page two of the sample pages later in this chapter.

Transitions such as: CUT TO, DISSOLVE, and FADE TO are not used in spec scripts because they indicate choices reserved for the director or editor.

Avoid CLOSE UP, LONG SHOT, AERIAL SHOT, SUPER SLOW MOTION, CAMERA PULLS BACK TO REVEAL, etc. in both scene headings and narrative descriptions because they indicate camera positions or director's choices.

You may see some of these transitions and camera placements in scripts that are available online but don't use them in your spec script. Chances are you are reading a shooting script which is why they are included.

Secondary scene headings are used when the primary location has not changed. For instance, Fisherman's Wharf is a location on the north shore of San Francisco; so, there is no need to be redundant with EXT. or DAY if they haven't changed.

FISHERMAN'S WHARF

The early afternoon activity around Fisherman's
Wharf seems relatively quiet. Some boats cruise
in the bay, a ferry of visitors heads toward
Alcatraz prison.

Notice the Master Scene Heading for the Golden Gate Bridge indicates it
is now NIGHT. Therefore, I needed to have a complete scene heading.

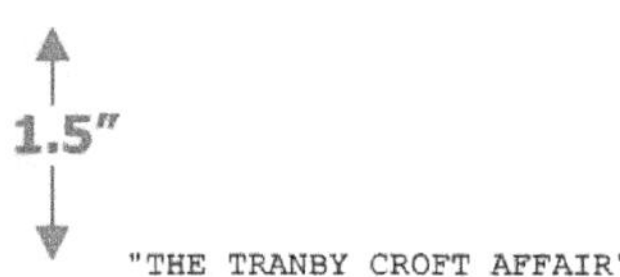

"THE TRANBY CROFT AFFAIR"

FADE IN:

EXT. SAN FRANCISCO - DAY

Fog partially covers The Golden Gate Bridge. The fog moves
fast toward the San Francisco skyline.

FISHERMAN'S WHARF

The early afternoon activity around Fisherman's Wharf seems
relatively quiet. Some boats cruise in the bay, a ferry of
visitors heads toward Alcatraz prison.

COIT TOWER

Near Coit Tower some beautiful homes appear to teeter,
precariously perched on the hillsides.

CALIFORNIA STREET

A cable car carries people up the hill toward the Mark
Hopkins Hotel. Passersby stop to look at the unusual
transports.

POLK STREET

Gay men walk hand in hand, arm in arm. Some in drag, others
wear leather and chains.

EXT. THE GOLDEN GATE BRIDGE - NIGHT

As darkness falls, crowds stroll onto the bridge.

FIRE DEPARTMENT BOATS

The fog lifts enough for literally thousands of spectators to
see three fireboats as they start spraying rainbow colored
streams of water from all seven nozzles. The crowd cheers
the traditional fourth of July celebration as San Francisco's
finest turns the show into a colorful water ballet.

A fireworks display spells out "4th of July" then disappears
into smoke. The crowd cheers again.

JAPAN CENTER

The Pagoda looms large above bare streets. The lights of
Japan Center shine bright and the streets fill with more
people moving about. Three tourists enter a restaurant.

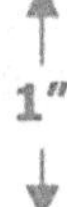

Page Two

The page number is positioned ½" from the top and 1.5" from the right edge.

You might also use a character name as a secondary scene heading or use terms like; LATER or ANOTHER ANGLE or FAVORING TRANBY.

The first time a character is seen, you'll need a description which should include three things:

1.   NAME (in all caps)
2.   Age
3.   A few lines or words that give the reader the essence of the character

Start by looking at your notes from Scene 2, Characters, Getting to Know Yours. You wrote a character Bio. Use it while typing the script. You should have identified complexes, phobias, pet peeves, fears, secrets, attitudes, beliefs, addictions, prejudices, inhibitions, frustrations, habits, superstitions, and moral stands.

Only describe physical traits such as height, weight, hair color, etc. if they are critical to the story.

Here are some examples:

```
Crime Illustrator TRANBY CROFT (28) sits
shoulders back, chest out, chin high in the front
row of the gallery. She dresses like a fashion
model, very attractive, feminine, and shapely
with an athletic body.
Her dark brown hair accentuates her perpetually
smiling face. Her eyes, translucent teal, the
most unique shade imaginable, mesmerize.
```

A student of mine wrote this wonderful description:

```
MISS SARAH, 70ish volunteer tidies up the already
neat reception desk.  She wears a pink jacket
smattered in a collection of service pins.
```

One of my favorite authors is Dean Koontz. Here is how he introduces Little Ozzie in *Odd Thomas:*

```
LITTLE OZZIE, a 400-pound man with six fingers on
his left hand.
```

Here is another example of how Koontz incorporates the first few lines of dialogue to enhance the character description (adapted to screenplay format):

STORMY LLEWELLYN, her uniform includes pink
shoes, white socks, a hot-pink skirt, a matching
pink-and-white blouse, and a perky pink cap.
With her Mediterranean complexion, jet-black
hair, and mysterious dark eyes, she looks like a
sultry espionage agent who had gone undercover as
a hospital candy striper.

                    STORMY
          When I have my own shop, the
          employees won't have to wear stupid
          uniforms.

                    ODD
          I think you look adorable.

                    STORMY
          I look like a Goth Gidget.

EXT. BUCHANAN STREET - NIGHT

MARTIN MAYHEW (45) moves slowly in the shadows near Japan
Center. His mouth opens slightly, his breath visible in the
cool night air. He moves on an apparently aimless course. He
looks average; average build, average height, average
everything.

EXT. OTAFUKU TEI RESTAURANT - REAR DOOR - NIGHT

The back door to the Japanese restaurant swings open and a
tiny man MARIKU YAMASHIRA (60) steps out. A tiny woman, MRS.
YAMASHIRA (55) follows. They wear dinner attire; he in a
suit, she in a cocktail dress.

He weaves like a drunk and she says so. They chatter in
Japanese. The woman throws her hands up and storms back into
the restaurant.

MARTIN

steps out of the shadows. He pulls a .45 caliber hand gun
from his waist band, aims at Mariku Yamashira, and pulls the
trigger.

MARIKU YAMASHIRA

looks surprised when the shell hits him. He reaches for his
chest and sees blood on his shirt. Martin fires another shot
which hits Yamashira in the head. It explodes blood all over
the wall and forces him into a garbage pile. He dies, eyes
open, lifeless.

INT. POLICE STATION - FIELDS' OFFICE - DAY

DETECTIVE MITCHELL FIELDS (50) sits at his desk, drinks
coffee and stares at the mounds of paperwork which he faces
for the day. He looks like a cowboy, an old Texas Ranger
with gray hair. His face, weathered from years of police
work, appears older than his 50 years.

INSERT - RADIO

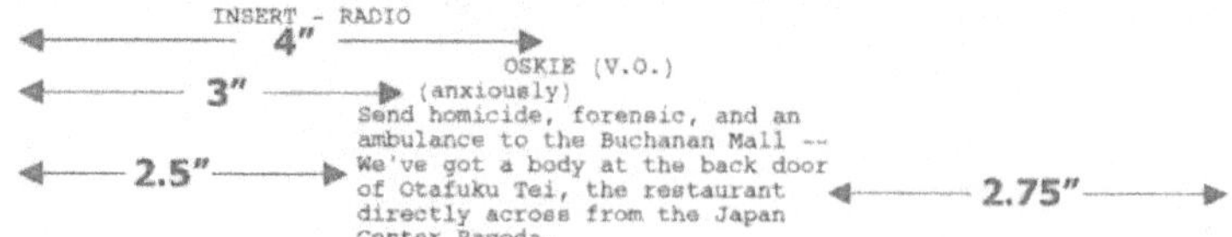

                         OSKIE (V.O.)
                    (anxiously)
          Send homicide, forensic, and an
          ambulance to the Buchanan Mall --
          We've got a body at the back door
          of Otafuku Tei, the restaurant
          directly across from the Japan
          Center Pagoda.

When dialogue is required, the character name comes first, centered at 4"
from the left margin. Then, actor directions in parenthesis, starting at 3" from the
left edge. Use parentheticals only when the actor would not know how to perform
it. In the example below, "Okay, boss" could be delivered with anger, sarcasm,
respect, humor, etc. Since it's not obvious, use a parenthetical to let the actor know
how you want it performed. The dialogue starts at 2.5" from the left edge and ends
at 2.75" from the right edge. Try to keep it snappy, one or two lines only (**5 max.**).
Such as:

                              ROSS
                    (sourly)
              Okay, boss.

Off screen dialogue, abbreviated (O.S.) indicates the actor is in the scene,
but the camera is on another actor, written like this:

                         ROSS (O.S.)
                    (sourly)
              Okay, boss.

Voice over, abbreviated (V.O.) means the person speaking is not in the
scene. This device can be used for a variety of reasons such as:

- when a narrator is describing the scene
- when the central character tells the story in 1st person
- when a secondary character is speaking through a
  telephone or radio.

The INSERT you see at the bottom of page two indicates the camera is on
the RADIO. The only thing on screen is an inanimate object. Use INSERT for
letters, newspaper clippings, clocks, etc. After the INSERT, you need another slug
line; such as, BACK TO FIELDS. You may use BACK TO SCENE or an entirely
different slug line which would indicate you're not going back to the original scene,
but to another place like EXT. CRIME SCENE – NIGHT.

INSERT – RADIO

                         OSKIE (V.O.)
                    (anxiously)
              Send homicide, forensic, and an
              ambulance to the Buchanan Mall ...
              We've got a body at the back door of
              Otafuku Tei, the restaurant directly
              across from the Japan Center Pagoda.

BACK TO FIELDS

As he pushes the reports aside, reaches for the phone, and dials the garage.

                    FIELDS
          This is Fields. Bring my car
          around please.

He pulls on his overcoat, switches off the lights, and leaves his office.

Beats are important in pacing a scene, but don't write the word "beat." You may see scripts online that put the word (beat) in parenthesis in dialogue to indicate the actor should pause before reading the next line. Instead, write a direction in parenthesis to give the actor some action, for example, (looks around the room).

In a screenplay, a beat occurs when the character's behavior changes or there is an emotional turn from positive to negative.

The INTERCUT is another cinematic convention I like to use. Let's say I want to have a telephone conversation between Fields and the guy who runs the morgue. My intention in this scene is to cut back and forth between the two men. Here's how it would look on the page:

INTERCUT PHONE CONVERSATION - FIELDS' OFFICE/BYERS' MORGUE

                    FIELDS
          Fields.

               BYERS
          You better get down here.

                    FIELDS
          What is it?

               BYERS
          Get down here. You have to see this in
          person.

A MONTAGE is a great device to move the story along quickly to show the passage of time.

MONTAGE - THE FUNERAL RITUAL

-- The Priest reads the Sutra.

-- Mrs. Yamashira starts a procession to the casket. She clasps her hands in prayer, bows, and tosses incense into an urn. When the fresh incense hits the smoldering embers in the urn, it hisses and a puff of smoke rises from the urn. She clasps her hands together, prays, bows, and returns to her seat.

-- Osuka, Takayama, and the other Directors follow the same procedure in hierarchical order.

-- The Priest chants and finishes the Sutra.

-- Osuka, Takayama, and four other Directors hoist the casket and march it outside the temple to the hearse.

-- The pallbearers unload the casket at the crematorium and deliver it to the metal rack which allows the casket to slide right up to the cremation chamber door.

-- The attendant hands Mrs. Yamashira a key, which she in turn hands to Osuka.

-- The family leaves to have the funeral banquet.

       A SERIES OF SHOTS is like a MONTAGE, but tells a story. Here is an example:

INT. POLICE STATION - ANOTHER OFFICE - DAY

Tranby and Mrs. Lee sit alone in a vacant office. Tranby tries to make Mrs. Lee feel safe. She uses a non-threatening interview method. Tranby starts to make sketches.

SERIES OF SHOTS - TRANBY CONSTRUCTS A PORTRAIT

A)   Tranby asks Mrs. Lee about basic head shape.

B)   The face starts to appear.

C)   They sit side-by-side, Tranby adds hair to the sketch.

D)   Tranby tacks the drawing to the wall and they examine it.

E)   Finally, Mrs. Lee approves the sketch.

There are other devices you may use for special circumstances; such as, superimposing dates or places, how to have two people talking at the same time, how to use foreign languages, etc., but these should suffice for now.

I highly recommend getting a copy of David Trottier's *Dr. Format Tells All*. It is a collection of all the columns he wrote for *Script* magazine from 1997 – 2012. It literally covers formatting from A-Z, Abbreviations to Wrylies. Okay, so A-W. It is a handy, easy to use reference and should be by your side as you write.

Your Turn

Complete the following exercises:
1. Look for the script of your favorite movie at:
    http://www.script-o-rama.com/table.shtml
2. Also, look for scripts of a similar genre and read as many as possible. Study the formatting as described in this Scene.

Sequence Two
First Draft

Scene 5

Writing Act I

> Micro-tension is the moment-by-moment tension that keeps the reader in a constant state of suspense over what is happening, not in the story, but in the next few seconds.
>
> – Donald Maass *The Fire in Fiction*

Balance

It's now time to start writing Act I. Let's first recap what needs to happen in the first 25-30 pages.

On page one, my preference is to show the audience the setting (time and place), establish a tone or mood, and define the pace. You may wish to start with a dramatic scene involving the Protagonist or show the Antagonist committing the crime. What's most important here is to engage the audience immediately.

By page three, the audience should know what the film is about and be hooked. The hook for TCA is the murder, which occurs on page two. On page three the lead detective is notified and heads to the crime scene to start the investigation.

Most audience members will decide no later than ten minutes into the film whether they care about the Protagonist or care what happens next. If they don't care, you've lost them. They will either leave the theatre, or stay and prepare ammunition to criticize the show later. Therefore, by page ten the audience should know what the story's about, where this story is going, whose story it is, what's at stake, and at least a hint at the Premise. From page four through page ten of TCA, the audience will meet the team of detectives and learn about their personalities as well as the preliminary evidence of the crime, be introduced to the victim's wife, and present the central character, Tranby Croft, in her work environment.

From page ten to the Disturbance you might identify goals, desires, needs that are universal and allude to the Achilles Heel, the Protagonist's flaw that must be overcome by the end of the story. The Balance from pages eleven to twenty-nine is used to introduce secondary characters. In TCA, we meet the morgue supervisor, the eye witness, the Bay-Tips news anchor, and the future love interest along with his sister. You may want to refer to the premise, create a mood, or introduce thematic devises, as I did with background of the victim and the intrigue of the victim's family business.

Disturbance

What happens that forces the hero to react and change goals for the rest of the story? This could take place on one page or be a series of scenes starting just before the 25% mark. In my case, it's a one-page set-up that ends when the Antagonist calls Tranby on the phone and threatens her.

Writing the Scene

As you write the scene, there are several tips to keep in mind. These guidelines will apply to all scenes in all three acts and they include:

- **Purpose** – Review the scene card and determine the purpose of the scene. Brainstorm ways of accomplishing that purpose. For instance, ask "How could my lovers meet?" Then list at least 10 options (more is better) and choose one you've never seen on film before.

- **Plan the Characterization** – On the scene card, you wrote the emotion to be acted. How will you reveal that emotion? Remember in a screenplay you cannot write thoughts or feelings. If I want Tranby to demonstrate confidence, I'll show strong posture "Shoulders back, chest out, chin high." Another resource you might want nearby is *The Emotion Thesaurus* by Angela Ackerman and Becca Puglisi. It lists 75 emotions and dozens of physical signals for each. In the case of "confidence," there are 38 options.

- **Show Don't Tell** – This is the mantra of filmmakers everywhere. Rather than having someone tell Tranby, "You sure have a lot of confidence." Show her displaying it with strong posture, walking with wide steps, winking or giving a self-assured nod, holding her hands steeple style when speaking, etc.

- **Scene Structure** – Just as a play has three Acts, each scene has a beginning, middle, and end. The beginning is the set-up or Balance of the scene, the middle is where the conflict happens, and the end is the resolution. On your scene cards, you wrote an opening value and a closing value. Therefore, you already know generally if it opens positively or negatively and the ending is the opposite of the beginning. Now think about the conflict. What will happen to make Tranby go from feeling safe to fearing for her life?

- **Conflict** – Every scene must have tension either through dialogue or action. In dialogue, you might use sarcasm, direct argument, or threats. In action, you could show someone stalking another, a fist fight, or a character rushing to beat a deadline. To learn more about this most important element, Donald Maass explains it well in his book, *The Fire in Fiction,* Chapter 8.

- **Subtext** – Avoid writing "on the nose" dialogue. A character shouldn't say everything explicitly. If a character says, "Are you almost done?" there is surely some anxiety in those words. Whatever the hidden meaning, it should be understood by the audience. The character's lines might insinuate, imply, or suggest multiple meanings. Linda Seger has an entire book on *Writing Subtext* using words, gestures and action, images and metaphors, and genre.

- **Active Voice** – Keep in mind your first audience is going to be a reader in a producer's office. The theatre audience won't get a chance to see your fine film if it isn't accepted by a reader. So, job one is to engage that first reader. Consider this description from Dean Koontz's *Relentless,* "The river runs red under the stain of sunset. Ripples, whorls, and lapping wavelets imply that exotic forms of life swarm under the surface." If your narrative fills the page with vivid images like that, your reader will be engaged which increases the probability of your success. Avoid passive construction like, "We see the sunset reflecting in the river. It is rippling from the sea creatures under the surface."

- **Think Through Transitions** – The end of one scene should lead to the beginning of the next. Ask a question at the end of scene five and answer it at the beginning of scene six. Make a statement like, "What moron would do that?" Then cut to the moron. Use a prop like a knife to end scene nine and show it in use to start scene ten.

Your Turn

Complete the following exercises:
1. Plan the Characterization of the scenes in Act I.
2. Write Act I.

Scene 6

Writing Act II

We will do anything to change until we start to; then we do everything to stop it.

> — Viki King *How to Write a Movie in 21 Days*

Act II

If you've ever had the need to diet, you have probably experienced the yo-yo effect. You lose weight, then you gain it back, then lose it again, but you always find it. Change scares us; so, we sabotage ourselves. Just before you reach your target weight, you fall off. This is what must happen in Act II. The Protagonist's goal is hard. It cannot be reached easily or there is no story, no drama.

Act II is 50% of the film's length, approximately 60 pages in our model. This can seem overwhelming; so, let's break it down into manageable chunks. I like to think in 15 page (minute) increments.

The Plan

Use the first 15 pages of Act II to disclose the Plan. Immediately following the Disturbance, the Hero has a dilemma – how to respond? Psychologists tell us that humans go through at least five stages of grief before accepting a situation and acting. The same holds true for decision-making. Few of us hear the facts and make an immediate decision, especially if the facts are life threatening. What will your character's reaction be: shock, fear, depression, anger, denial, etc.? Show your hero going through the decision-making process to accept the task ahead. While Tranby is startled by the phone call, she remains in denial. She rationalizes, if the threat were legitimate, Martin wouldn't call. He'd make face-to-face contact.

The Obstacles

I typically try to put in an obstacle at three points in Act II. For the first draft, let's say they occur at pages 45, 60, and 75.

Write the awareness scene. Although Tranby is in denial, at some point she should admit to herself that the threat is real and act. I chose to have Martin and Aaron break into Tranby's apartment and wait for her. When she gets home with Harris and sees the door has been jimmied, Harris calls the police. Martin and Aaron sneak out the back to avoid arrest but this is too close for comfort and Tranby must accept the truth. She's being stalked.

Pages 45-60

Obstacles are challenging but because she can overcome them, they make her more confident. Tranby grows, becomes smarter, knows that the next challenge will be overcome through creativity and use of skills learned along the journey. Tranby learns that Harris might be a suspect based upon his past dealings with the SFPD. When Harris leaves Tranby's apartment, Ross tails him. After talking to Harris, Tranby feels conflicted. Should she trust Fields or Harris?

The Midpoint – Page 60

At the midpoint, your hero makes a commitment to the Plan. There is no turning back now.

In the classic *Gone with the Wind*, Scarlett says, "As God is my witness, as God is my witness they're not going to lick me. I'm going to live through this and when it's over, I'll never be hungry again. No, nor any of my folk. If I have to lie, steal, cheat or kill. As God is my witness, I'll never go hungry again."

If you wrote that today, it would be criticized as being "on-the-nose" dialogue, telling not showing, and breaking the fourth wall because she's talking to the audience not another actor.

Symbolically, have your character complete Scarlett's statement: "As God is my witness, I will ___________________________________." Then determine how you will show not tell it.

For example, at the midpoint of *Absence of Malice,* Paul Newman doesn't say, "As God is my witness, I'm going to set-up Rosen and the others and make them pay…." He goes to his Uncle's house and says, "I got a job to do. I need some information on Elliot Rosen." Then, there is a sequence of scenes where he buys an answering machine and sets it up, goes to the bank and gets a cashier's check made out to the "Committee for a Better Miami," then meets with D.A. Quinn and says, "I want a deal…." We know by his actions he's setting the stage to get his revenge.

In TCA, Tranby makes a commitment to take Harris' advice and hide.

Pages 60-75

At the page 60 plot point, the hero faces an obstacle contrary to her goal value. If she's fighting for justice, at page 60 she should confront injustice.

You could add more Obstacles. In Tranby's case, she's required to figure out how to escape the watchful eyes of Ross who is camped out in front of her apartment.

Perhaps self-doubt sets in. She didn't think it was going to be this difficult. Just before page 75, the hero is just about to give up. This injustice thing is just too much and she feels she cannot win.

Page 75

Then something happens. She thinks of a creative way around the dilemma. Harris gets arrested for obstruction of justice and although it's not seen in the script, Tranby moves to a new location in Carmel.

Her brain switches from problem analysis to identifying alternative solutions.

Pages 75-90

Now the story is moving quite rapidly. The scenes should be logical and flow in a cause and effect manner. The effect of scene 29 is the cause of scene 30, etc. The action builds in intensity until you reach the Crisis.

I chose to have these scenes be about the investigation. Fields, Ross, and McNally go to Martin's house and learn he is a serial killer. Fields must go to the Otafuku Tei restaurant and tell Mrs. Yamashira that her son was also killed by Martin.

The Crisis

At page 90, the hero faces the end of the line, the "all is lost" scene. The forces of antagonism are so great that the audience thinks it's over. The hero cannot win. She faces antagonism even greater than injustice. She faces tyranny.

Harris is followed when he gets out of jail. Tranby feels high anxiety. They are going to have to run again.

Subplots

The purpose of a subplot is to add dimension to the script. In the first draft of TCA, I had the main plot regarding the murder and Tranby's connection to it, and a romantic subplot involving Harris. It was clear that the script was one dimensional. Therefore, in the rewrites I added more details about the victim's family and more details about the investigation by Fields' team.

If you haven't started a subplot by now, the second act is a good place to begin one. The second act is long and will become boring if the only conflict is between the Protagonist and the Antagonist. Adding another dimension will maintain audience interest.

You may have more than one subplot but the more subplots you create, the more complex your story will become and the harder it will be to manage. *L.A. Confidential,* for instance, had eight plot lines in the novel. The screenwriters reduced it to three. When I read the book, after seeing the movie, I was totally confused.

Most films have one or two subplots. Few have more than five. A good subplot does:

- ➢ Move the story onward or in a different direction
- ➢ Help prove the premise of the story
- ➢ Expose the main character's traits or flaws
- ➢ Disclose what a character values or desires
- ➢ Explain why and how a character transforms

A poor subplot does not:
- ➢ Conform to basic dramatic structure
- ➢ Traverse the main plot
- ➢ Have any bearing on the story
- ➢ Precede the main plot

Subplot Design

You'll need to create scene cards for the subplots. The number of scenes will depend upon your specific need. I wrote four sequences for the love story, eight scenes for the investigation, and seven scenes for the crime family, which contradicts the premise. The premise of TCA is *Justice will prevail….* In the "B" subplot the crime family's premise is that *Crime pays….* When these two intersect, the greatest conflict occurs and therefore the drama is heightened.

In any event, you'll need at least four scenes for each subplot. Namely:
1. Hook
2. Disturbance (Plot Point I)
3. Crisis (Plot Point II)
4. Climax

See my example on the next page.

TRANBY PLOT LINES

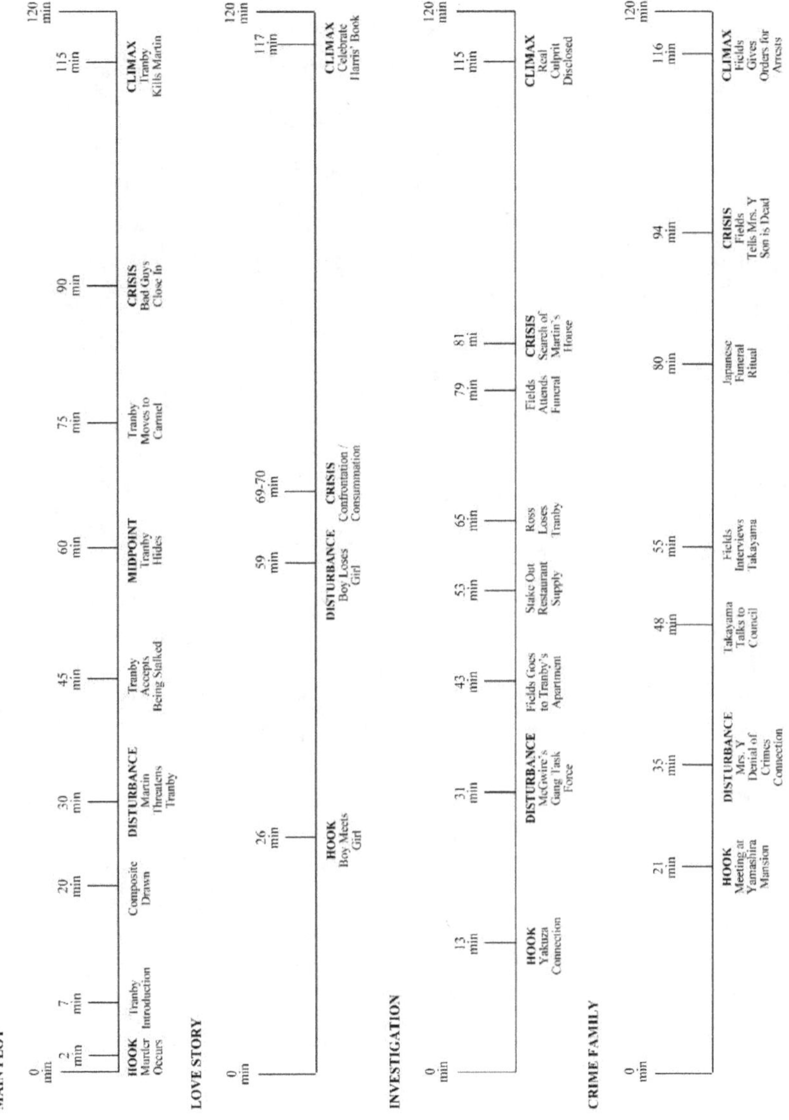

Your Turn

Complete the following exercises:

1. Determine if you need more subplots.
    a. Draw plot lines for the subplots of your story.
    b. Prepare scene cards for additional subplots.
2. Write Act II.

Scene 7

Writing Act III

If the scene is about what the scene is about, you're in deep
s#*&.

– Robert McKee STORY

Act III

Act III is the last 25% of the film's length, approximately 30 pages. This
is where you must tie-up all daggling strings. Everything must be resolved or the
audience will feel let down. Try to include at least three scenes or sequences that
accomplish the most import audience requirements. I need to know:

1. Did the Protagonist win, loose, draw?
2. Do I feel satisfied? (I don't like ambiguous endings)
3. Are there any unresolved issues?

The Climax – Pages 91 - 105

Create the climactic scene (or sequence) that shows how the central
character handles the Crisis. Either the Protagonist wins the competition by
defeating the Antagonist, loses to the Antagonist and doesn't get the prize, or
succeeds by giving up something of greater value leading to an ironic resolution.
This is where you will show how the central character has grown, how the lesson
was learned, how the premise was proven.

Tranby devises a plan of action to find out what Melinda Gary knows about
the murder. Harris kidnaps Melinda and interrogates her. Martin shows up and
Tranby mortally wounds him.

Pages 106 – 115

Ask yourself, have I started something that has not been finished? The
audience wants to know the final direction for all subplots.

In the first draft of TCA, I had McNally go undercover near the middle of
Act II. When the movie ended, I realized he hadn't been seen since. So, I wrote a
scene at this point where he stumbled out of one of the Yakuza brothels. He looked

like he had been on a three-day toot and all he said was, "Whew!" The audience needs to know what happened to McNally.

In the final draft, I cut the undercover angle. I decided to have Martin look at Fields and in his dying breath disclose the real culprit. This will be important when you start to rewrite, because you are going to want to explore twists and surprises. Having a plot turn near the end can be quite enjoyable for the audience. More on this in Scene 9, Polishing Techniques.

The Outcome – Pages 116 – 120

The Outcome or new Balance in many of the better films is a mirror image of the opening image. My favorite example of this is in *Burn After Reading.* The movie starts with a Zoom-In on Earth, moves to a long shot of the United States, and into the CIA. The movie ends with a Zoom-Out from the CIA, to the United States, and ends on the Earth. An exact mirror image.

I chose to end TCA by duplicating the Boy-Meets-Girl scene.

Dialogue

McKee says write dialogue last, meaning he writes the narrative or action components without the characters' speaking. Then, he goes back and inserts dialogue where it is necessary. "Where necessary" means only write discourse to enhance the cinematic image, when the audience might not get it without the interchange. Theoretically, you should finish the narrative for Act III then go back and supplement speeches where they are essential.

I advise my students to strive for a 2 to 1 ratio. That is twice as much narrative as dialogue. Film is a visual medium. In fact, many screenwriting professors suggest that if a film is well written, you could turn off the sound and still know what's happening in the story. We did, after all, start with silent movies.

While I understand the theory, I find it tough to avoid all dialogue. If you find that difficult, don't worry about it. The ground rules for dialogue have been mentioned previously but it's worth repeating. Here are some guidelines:

- Keep dialogue focused on revealing character, conflict, or emotion.
- Keep it short, one or two lines, five at the most.
- Keep it conversational, but avoid "Hi, how you doin'?" "Fine, and you?"

Polish and Tighten Dialogue

The best dialogue is quotable. My family recently played a game texting quotes of movie dialogue that made us think of the film without using the title. Can you name the films from these quotes?

"You had me at 'Hello.'"
"You can't handle the truth."
"There's no crying in baseball."
"I'll be back."
"I'll have what she's having."
"Go ahead, make my day."
"I ate his liver with some fava beans and a nice Chianti."
"Toto, I have a feeling we're not in Kansas anymore."
"You're gonna need a bigger boat."
"I'm not bad, I'm just drawn that way."

We use it to express ourselves. Some of us even try to imitate the vocal tones of the actor who spoke it. I'm not suggesting that you spend hours hunting for the line you think will be imitated for years after your fine movie has been produced. No, just write it to express the needs of the character in the scene at the time. Here are some thoughts to keep in mind.

Make it Entertaining

Exceptional dialogue is like music or poetry. Aristotle's paradigm for dramatic structure included six elements; Plot (order), Theme (premise), Character (personality of the players), Diction (dialogue), Music (rhythm or melody of speeches), and Spectacle (scenery, costumes, and special effects).

Diction and Music augment the other components. It is not idle chat. It must be used sparingly to:

- ➢ Express the premise
- ➢ Reveal character
- ➢ Imply character growth and change
- ➢ Clarify the characters' goals, dreams, or traits

External vs. Internal Dialogue

By definition, dialogue is the external expression of an internal thought or emotion. In some scenes, you will want to provide some exposition and describe things like who this character is, what the character's job is, when events are taking place and deadlines, where the action is, how the character should accomplish the task, and sometimes why the job is necessary or why it's important for this character.

One of the most important things I learned from Sam Havens was to use questions to trigger intrigue and tension. Tension occurs when the Outcome is in doubt. In the TCA script, Fields arrives at the crime scene after Ross and McNally, so he uses who, what, when, where questions to find out what they already know.

Usually in the Balance, Disturbance, and especially in the Plan, a character may use dialogue to state an intention. Actors are looking for the character's objective. What is the character's motivation? Even the minor ones must have an intention, as Fields does when he tells Mrs. Yamashira, "… I will do everything in my power to bring whoever did this to justice." I particularly like using intention statements as transitions to the next scene. State the intention and carry it out in the next scene.

Most professions have a certain jargon which is used to exclude people not in the "in-crowd." Cops use procedural terms, chaplains speak in biblical verbiage, a medical examiner would list the cause of death as "asphyxiation" while I might say "he was smothered."

The specific vocabulary, phonology, and grammar used creates a distinct dialect for each character. You don't want your characters to sound alike.

Internal dialogue is that voice only you can hear. It's the subconscious mind talking to your conscious mind. The problem with internal dialogue is the audience cannot hear it. Therefore, it shouldn't be used in a screenplay.

There are two ways to convey internal thoughts or feelings in a screenplay; voiceover or subtext. I did not use the voiceover technique for internal secrets and fears in TCA because I think it's lazy. I want to encourage you to allow the actor to act thoughts and feelings through your narrative descriptions or subtext. If you can't think of a way for the actor to express thoughts or feelings then use voiceover, but it should be used sparingly. Here is an example of what I could have done when Harris first meets Tranby:

```
Harris looks up, makes eye contact, pauses and tries not
to smile like men do when lust destroys their brains.
His eyes sparkle as he gazes upon Tranby Croft for the
first time.

                    HARRIS (V.O.)
          The object of my most passion-
          ate desires stands before me.

He extends his hand in a business-like greeting.

                    HARRIS
          Harris Richardson, pleased to
          meet you.
```

Your Turn

Complete the following exercises:

1. Scan your script for opportunities to polish and tighten dialogue.
2. Finish the first draft.

Sequence Three
Final Draft

Scene 8

Strategies for Rewriting

> Actually, *Come Blow Your Horn* took a year to write and two and a half years to rewrite. I did twenty-two complete versions, starting on page 1 and finishing on page 125 every time, and almost never did I repeat myself.
>
> – Neil Simon *Rewrites*

Strategies for Rewriting

You now have a first draft of your screenplay. I suggest you let it rest. How long will depend upon how patient you are. At least a few weeks will get your mind off the story. During your hiatus, read a novel of a different genre or better yet read a business book like *Achieving on Purpose: Your GUIDE to Managerial Success.*

In a month or so, follow these four steps:

1. Read your first draft
2. Reflect on what you have written
3. Analyze the script
4. Write the second draft

Read Your First Draft

There are several reading options. The best and most fun option is to have a "living room reading" in which you recruit several people to assume roles and read it out loud. You'll need enough actors to cover the three to five main characters plus a narrator. If you have a cast of thousands, you'll need to double-up on the acting assignments. I recommend that you NOT be one of the readers. It's important for you to hear what it sounds like. Was the dialogue musical? Are the narrative descriptions vivid? Is it entertaining? Etc. You may also invite others to be in the audience and ask for their feedback. Make it a party but remember you need specific feedback. Finally, record the reading and the feedback. That way you'll be able to go back and listen to it again and finetune your notes.

A second group option would be to use a writer's group. I've attended two in Dallas. The Dallas Screenwriters Association (DSA) has scene reads the last Tuesday of every month. Members may have up to 10 pages read. Find out more at https://www.dallasscreenwriters.com/scene-reads. The down side to this option is only 10 pages are read. The up side is the DSA brings in working actors to read. The North Dallas Screenwriting Group has a critique session every other Monday in Richardson, Texas. Once you have attended several meetings, you will become eligible to have a complete script beak-down. Learn more here https://www.meetup.com/north-dallas-screenwriters/. Not in Dallas? Look for a Screenwriters Association or Meetup near you.

The third option is to give a copy of the script to several friends. Ask each to read the script and provide feedback. Ideally, these readers should know a bit about writing. I use people who have been through my classes and who know how to give useful feedback. If you have no friends, or no friends with credentials, you can coach them or provide a list of questions you'd like answered.

Effective feedback is specific and sincere. Ask your readers to try to avoid value judgments like: "This is an excellent piece of work" or, "This sucks!" Rather, ask them to be specific about what they've read relative to some skill or technique you are learning and why it worked, in their opinion.

Things to focus on would be structural items like the Disturbance, Crisis, etc., or characterization items like a person's flaw. Was the dialogue realistic? Was there enough conflict? Did the scene turn? etc.

If the readers are not familiar with this jargon, then ask them to answer specific questions like:

- When were you most engaged?
- When were you least engaged?
- Where was the most tension?
- Where do I need more tension?
- Which characters were most believable?
- Which characters were not believable?
- When were you surprised in the story?
- Where was it too predictable?
- What did you like most?
- Would you have me change anything?

As you receive the feedback, insist on specifics. Here are two examples of feedback I gave to a student. The first is positive and the second is corrective.

For positive feedback, state *What* specifically you liked and *Why* you liked it. For example:

What = "When you bring Melody into the club wearing a hooded cape."

Why = "It's a nice touch. Hiding her identity adds intrigue to the scene."

For corrective feedback state *What* you disliked, offer an Alternative Positive Behavior (*APB*), and explain *Why* your idea might have a more favorable result. NEVER simply criticize. There's no such thing as constructive *criticism*. If it's constructive, it isn't critical and if it's critical, it isn't constructive. Rather, use an unconditionally constructive process. For example:

What = "When you wrote, 'Roscoe stares at the food.' Then you cut to
        EXT. CLINIC – BACK FIELD seems abrupt to me."

APB = "You might want to put in something more between Mirian and
        Roscoe before the cut. Like, 'Eat up, Honey, I'll be right back.'"

Why = "That way the audience will get the sense a transition is about to
        happen."

The last option is for you to read the script aloud to yourself. It's hard to be objective about your own work, but it is doable. I would suggest that you do a scene-by-scene analysis which is explained below.

Reflect on What you have Written

Reflection is an essential part of learning and increasing professional effectiveness. In this context, reflection is about assessing where you began, where you are, and where you are going. Viki King suggests we write the first draft from the heart and the second draft from the head. Now is the time to get inside your head.

You have just heard your first draft read in your living room, received the feedback from your friends, or finished reading it aloud to yourself. Think about it for a day. What did you learn?

After the day of reflection, write down the answers to these questions:

1. Why did I want to write a story about this subject?
2. How well did this first draft accomplish the goal?
3. What do I have to do now to fix what's not working?

Analyze the Script

This is a useful step regardless of how you got your feedback. It's crucial if you're the only one reading your script.

To find the flaws, break each scene down into its beats. A beat is a single intention carried out. The first thing a director looks for is beats. In a screenplay, a beat occurs when the character's behavior changes or there is an emotional turn from positive to negative. Then, with the Premise in mind, determine if the scene is a true event. Ask, Does the scene turn? Have I used subtext? Is the conflict appropriate and what I intended? What else might not be working? Let's look at the first draft of my Boy-Meets-Girl scene.

In my Boy-Meets-Girl scene, I wanted to start with Harris outside Tranby's apartment. He rings the buzzer and talks with her over the intercom. He is professional, like a salesman, trying to get an appointment. She is busy and doesn't want company but lets him enter the building. When she opens her apartment door, he is immediately smitten. This is love at first sight for Harris but not for Tranby. She is still cautious. She's more focused on meeting her deadline. They talk while she works and she becomes suspicious of his motives and asks why he has come to her. He discloses that Melinda Gary gave her credit as the illustrator on the air. He asks her what she thinks of his idea and she reacts about Melinda being unprofessional. He presses the issue of working together and she starts to negotiate. The scene ends when she finishes the drawings and invites him to come to the studio with her to turn in her drawings.

So, you might synopsize the beats like this:

1. Approaching her/ignoring him
2. Smitten with her/rejecting him
3. Building rapport/hiding her suspicions
4. Selling himself/angry with Melinda
5. Closing the sale/steaming over Melinda
6. Stating his case/negotiating with him
7. He's made an advance/she's leading him on

What follows are the first six pages of the Boy-Meets-Girl sequence. I have marked the separation of where the first four beats start. See if you can identify where the last three beats start. Then describe what flaws exist and what you would do about them. Consider how you would rewrite these pages to make them more entertaining or believable.

INT. TRANBY'S APARTMENT - STUDIO - DAY

Tranby sits at her art table developing some drawings for the
BayTips show. The doorbell rings. She gets up and starts for
the door... Stops... adds just a little more color to the
sketch... hesitates then proceeds to the door occasionally
looks back at the drawing. She presses the speaker button.

EXT. TRANBY'S BUILDING

Harris Richardson stands at the front door. Tranby's voice
comes through the speaker.

                    TRANBY (O.S.)
          Who is it?

                    HARRIS
          Harris Richardson... I'm a
          writer... I'd like to talk to you.

                    TRANBY (O.S.)
          Come up to the third floor. It's
          Suite 208.

                    HARRIS
               (mumbling barely audible)
          Third floor? #208?

The electronic lock buzzes. Harris opens the door and enters
the building.

INT. THIRD FLOOR HALLWAY

Just outside Tranby's apartment, Harris finishes his climb.
Tranby opens the door.

INT. TRANBY'S APARTMENT

Harris enters.

                    TRANBY
          You may come in, but I'm real busy.
          I've got a deadline to meet.

                    HARRIS
          What are you working on?

Tranby leads Harris down the hall to the studio.

Beat

1

                    TRANBY
          I'm doing sketches for BayTips.

                    HARRIS
          I've seen that... What's this
          particular case about?

Beat 2

TRANBY'S APARTMENT - STUDIO

During the subsequent scene, as Tranby explains the case, she
does it with her drawings. More or less the way that Melinda
Gary will do it on the air.

                    TRANBY
          About two weeks ago, these two boys
          were kidnapped.
               (shows drawing)
          Last night they were found buried
          in two oil drums near the Presidio.

Harris is enthralled by the presentation as she shows another
drawing.

                    TRANBY (CONT'D)
          What I'm trying to do with this
          drawing...
               (another sketch)
          is re-create a scene that would
          make a strong visual impact...
          something that would jog someone's
          memory.

ANOTHER ANGLE

Beat 3

                    HARRIS
          How can you re-create something
          that happened, when you weren't
          there. Indeed no one was there, at
          least that you can talk to.

                    TRANBY
          Good question... I did this by
          calling on my own emotions... I try
          to imagine what it would feel like
          to be kidnapped, driven to a remote
          location, and shot.

                    HARRIS
          Were they dead when put into the
          drums.

                    TRANBY
          I didn't ask, didn't want to
          know... I wouldn't use that
          information on the air anyway for
          the family's sake.

                    HARRIS
          Are these murders related to the
          Japanese man's murder the other
          night?

                    TRANBY
          As a matter of fact they are... How
          did you know that?

                    HARRIS
          Wishful thinking... but those boys
          are oriental.

                    TRANBY
               (cautiously now)
          Maybe you should tell me a little
          bit about yourself.

          Tranby continues working on the drawings, while Harris
          explains. Harris finds a comfortable chair.

Beat

4

                    HARRIS
          I write mystery and suspense
          novels, which are based on real
          life murders. I'd like to get your
          help in re-creating all the crimes
          that this guy has committed so I
          can write about this particular
          case.

                    TRANBY
          Why come to me?

                    HARRIS
          I've published five novels... Every
          time, I've gone to the police...
          The first two were very successful,
          in terms of my relationship with
          the police... During the third one
          I got some pretty incriminating
          evidence against a rather prominent
          detective... I published it as
          fiction, of course, but they didn't
          like the implications... During the
          writing of the last two they've
          been uncooperative, to say the
          least...
                    (MORE)

                    HARRIS (CONT'D)
          So, when the lady on Channel 2 gave
          you credit as the crime
          illustrator, I thought it would be
          a great angle on a new book...
          and...

                    TRANBY
          Wait a minute, did you say Melinda
          gave me credit?

                    HARRIS
          Yeah, so?

                    TRANBY
          She's not suppose to do that... Are
          you sure she mentioned my name?

                    HARRIS
          Absolutely, how do you think I
          found you?

                    TRANBY
          Well, I'm going to have a word with
          Ms. Melinda Gary.

                    HARRIS
          So, what do you think?

                    TRANBY
          I think it was terribly
          unprofessional.

                    HARRIS
          My coming here?

                    TRANBY
          What? No, Melinda mentioning my
          name on the air.

                    HARRIS
          What do you think about my
          proposal?

                    TRANBY
          I think it's interesting, but
          what's in it for me?

                    HARRIS
          The opportunity to work with a
          suave, debonair writer?

                    TRANBY
          Am I going to get paid for this?
          What about story credit?

                    HARRIS
          Well, I could give you a percentage
          of whatever I get. Deferred of
          course until, or if, I get paid
          anything.

                    TRANBY
          With five novels already published,
          you don't have a contract for your
          next?

                    HARRIS
          Not really, my publisher gets first
          refusal... but there is no money
          guarantee.

                    TRANBY
          Well, I think these are in pretty
          good shape... What do you think?

She holds up the finished sketches.

                    HARRIS
          They look great to me.

                    TRANBY
          Would you like to go to the studio
          with me? We could talk more about
          this proposal of yours.

                    HARRIS
          I'd love to.

INT. T.V. STUDIO - DAY

Harris and Tranby stand off stage and watch the crew prepare
the set.

Melinda enters the set. A crew member clips a microphone to
the inside of Melinda's blouse. She looks down at his hands
and then snaps up quickly at his eyes. Her look scolds him
for fondling her breast during the procedure.

Tranby storms onto the set.

                    DIRECTOR
          Tranby, clear the set... we have
          five seconds...

Tranby shoves a pointed finger into Melinda's nose.

                    TRANBY
          Don't you use my name again.

```
                    DIRECTOR
              four... three...

Melinda's brow furrows.

                    MELINDA
               (disgustedly)
          I won't...

                    DIRECTOR
          two... one...

Melinda snarls.

                    MELINDA
          For God Sake!

The Director points his finger at Melinda.

                    DIRECTOR
               (mouthing the words)
          You're on.

Melinda puts on that big Hollywood smile.

                    MELINDA
          Good evening... This is BayTips...
          I'm Melinda Gary.

Tranby and Harris watch from the side of the set as Melinda
begins her report faintly in the background.  Harris sees how
Tranby's drawings are changed by a crew member and shot by
another T.V. camera to stage left of Melinda.  A monitor in
front of Harris shows the magic of television, revealing what
actually goes out over the airwaves.

                    HARRIS
          Absolutely fascinating.

                    TRANBY
          Okay... I'll do it.

                    HARRIS
          You'll work with me?

                    TRANBY
          Sure... I've been thinking about it
          the whole time... It sounds like
          fun.
```

So, the first bit of feedback I received was that Tranby let Harris into her apartment without question, on page 19. No woman would allow a strange man into her apartment without knowing who he was or having met him in another context. What was I thinking?

The second thing you might have noticed is there is too much dialogue. From the bottom half of page 20 until the scene ends at page 23 is almost exclusively conversation. It reads more like a stage play than a screenplay.

Third, some of the dialogue violates the five-lines rule.

Your Turn

Complete the following exercises:

1.   Read your first draft.
2.   Reflect on what you have written.
3.   Analyze the script.
4.   Write the second draft.

Scene 9

Polishing Techniques

A Protagonist and his story can only be as intellectually fascinating and emotionally compelling as the forces of antagonism make them.

— Robert McKee *STORY*

Third Draft

After you complete the second draft of the script you will want to get another round of feedback. I recommend you chose a different method. For instance, if you read it by yourself, alone in the dark, then have a "living room reading" this time.

You might also want to consider a coverage from a professional reader or script consultant. A coverage is what Hollywood story analysts do for a living. They read scripts that are solicited by Producers and prepare a report (coverage) that consists of a synopsis, analysis, and a recommendation. The recommendation will be either go, no-go, or consider.

A script consultant will provide a more detailed evaluation and recommendations on how to improve the script.

When I provide a script consultation, I read the script and make general notes in the margins. Then, I go back through the script with a fine-toothed comb. My 10-point analysis includes the following:

1. Basic story structure
2. Conflict and action
3. Emotional impact
4. Characterization
5. Dialogue
6. Narrative description
7. Believability
8. Originality
9. Title
10. Commercial appeal

The script is returned with hand-written notes in the margin and a typed report of three to seven pages, based upon what needs work.

Once you have reflected on the second round of feedback, it's time to refine the script into showcase condition. I have mentioned these techniques in various chapters, but now you may need to revisit some of the more critical moments in the story and choose to use some or all of these polishing techniques:

- Raising the Level of Antagonism
- Adding Some Secrets or Twists
- Improving Character Dimension
- Ensuring a Character Arc
- Using Imagery
- Getting the Title Right

Begin with your Premise. You may want to perfect your premise, as I did, before rewriting. Egri says you may start your play without a premise or with one you feel is inadequate but, at some point, you will need to find THE moral premise. My new one is, "*Justice prevails when we stand up to wrongdoing and become truly brave.*"

Now, with the premise in mind, let's look at polishing the script.

Raising the Level of Antagonism

Indisputably, the most critical element to drama design is conflict. Your story needs to be a series of progressive complications. While each scene must have tension, some scenes will have more conflict than others. Raising the level of antagonism means reviewing the three major plot points to ensure they radically upset the main character's life. The Antagonist needs to be a worthy adversary.

Tranby represents justice. Therefore, her story's forces of antagonism must represent the negative values of justice; such as, dishonesty, injustice, or lawlessness. There are at least 25 degrees of negativity from bothered (mild) to blind rage (extreme). For purposes of screenwriting, let's use three degrees; assigning one for each plot point, and increasing magnitude to each from bad to worse to worst.

At the Disturbance (plot point I), write a scene that shows something bad happening to the Protagonist. This event must surprise, shock, or anger the audience; so, they feel empathy for the hero.

At the Mid-Point Conflict, write a scene that is worse. Now the audience is fuming with fear and anxiety.

At the Crisis (plot point II), write a scene that is the worst you can imagine. The audience must be horrified and hopeless. This is the end of the line, the "all is lost" moment. Hal Croasmun says, "Send your characters to Hell."

Now consider how you might rewrite those major plot points to raise the level of antagonism. Ask yourself, Have I truly taken the character to the limits? If this is a murder mystery, like TCA, the final confrontation will most likely be a face-to-face battle with the Antagonist in which the Protagonist must face death. If this is a psychological thriller, then the end of the line should be a mind-boggling dilemma. If this is a love story, then the lovers must feel antipathy. Whatever your premise is, the Crisis must be as far afield from it as possible.

Adding Some Secrets or Twists

When I think of the best twists, they usually come near the end of the movie. The twist is a devise to surprise the audience. On page 116 of TCA, in Martin's dying breath he discloses that Takayama hired him to kill Mr. Yamashira so Takayama would become head of the syndicate.

There are many examples of this in Hollywood. Spoiler Alert! One of my favorites was in *Planet of the Apes*. For the entire movie, we believe that three astronauts have crash landed on an unknown planet ruled by apes. In the final scene, Charlton Heston's character sees the Statue of Liberty; so, they were always on Earth but didn't know it. In *Psycho*, we believe Marion Crane is murdered by Norman Bate's Mother. Except in the end we find out Mom's been dead for years. In *Chinatown*, we find out a secret that Evelyn's sister is also her daughter. In the *Usual Suspects*, "Verbal" Kint is Keyser Soze. In *The Sixth Sense*, one of the dead people Cole sees is Dr. Malcolm Crowe.

The trick with twists and secrets is you must provide enough foreshadowing so the twist makes sense. Like in the *Sixth Sense*, Malcolm is always wearing the same clothes. Whenever Malcolm approaches a living person the air gets cold and we can see others' breath. Anna supposedly ignores Malcolm because she thinks he's a workaholic, and so on, until the end when Malcolm realizes he's dead and we smack our heads because we should have figured it out.

Neil Simon told of advice he'd received from Reginald Rose in his autobiography *Rewrites*. Rose said, "…You don't make characters exit to clear the stage. They have to have a life of their own offstage. When they come back, we want to know where they've been, and why they came back when they did and not some other time." To have a clear understanding of a character's motivation, you may want to create an outline of what devious things the pivotal character is doing when not on-screen.

Improving Character Dimension

This is a matter of going back to Scene 2, Characters, Getting to Know Yours and reviewing the cast design table. Have you revealed the characterization traits you intended to reveal?

Character is best defined by the response it makes to the environment. Sam Havens used to say, "Create hammers and find out what (your characters) say to that situation." In other words, has your supporting cast done its job to bring out the hero's true character. Have you thrown enough rocks? Are the rocks big enough?

Think oxymoron. Are your characters filled with contradictions? Did you disclose the main character's flaw and have her overcome it in the climactic scene?

Ensuring a Character Arc

While a Character Arc is not necessary, the best films have the Protagonist grow and change. This transformation doesn't happen in one scene. It takes the entire story to transform the character. For example:

- Michael Dorsey becomes a better man because he was forced to think and act like a woman in *Tootsie*.
- Oskar Schindler goes from materialism to humanism in *Schindler's List*.
- George Bailey goes from wanting to commit suicide to wanting to live again after seeing what life would have been like had he never been born in *It's a Wonderful Life*.
- Ripley doesn't want anything to do with those aliens but ends up becoming the hero in *Aliens*.
- Michael Corleone detaches himself from his family's business until he's slapped by Police Captain McCluskey; then, he ascends to the family throne in *The Godfather*.

When the story begins, the Protagonist has a flaw that is preventing him from being complete. When the story ends and he has transformed, the change has proven the premise. In TCA, Tranby must become brave. In the beginning, her flaw is naïveté and she lacks courage. But, it's not until she finds her courage that justice is served.

Sometimes, as in *The Godfather,* the transformation goes from positive to negative. Michael Corleone is virtuous in the beginning. He reassures Kay, "That's my family, Kay, it's not me." He transforms to villainous because his father is mortally wounded in an assassination attempt, and he learns to make people offers they can't refuse.

The transformation needs to be planned like all scenes. If you wish to include an arc, you'll need a minimum of four scenes, but more likely from seven to twelve.

Using Imagery

Imagery is a cinematic strategy of embedding symbolism or metaphor throughout the film. Hitchcock was a master at this. For example, *Psycho* uses bird symbolism in setting, character name, character hobby, and dialogue. The film begins in Phoenix, Arizona; the **Phoenix** is a mythological bird. Marion's last name is "**Crane**." Norman practices **taxidermy** as a hobby and his favorites are birds. Norman describes Marion's eating behavior as "eats like a bird.".

In *Vertigo,* Hitchcock uses spirals as symbols of the acrophobia suffered by the main character. From the theatrical poster, which shows a body spinning inside spirals, to the opening credits where a spiral emerges from a woman's eye, to the dolly-zoom which created disorientation, to Kim Novak's hair style, to the winding stairs of the bell tower.

In *The Sixth Sense,* the color red is seen on anything tainted by the other world. Cole and Anna wear costumes of red, the red balloon rises through the staircase, Kyra's get well soon card is written in red, and the red door knob to the cellar.

Directors use many methods to create a mood, elicit an emotion, or produce a reaction from the audience. They use camera lenses, camera position, camera motion, and lighting, among other technical choices. These are decisions you should leave up to the director. On the other hand, you can allude to a technique you'd like the director to use via color, props, wardrobe suggestions, locations, and the natural environment.

Getting the Title Right

Once you have polished the script to the best of your ability, there is one last thing to do. Review your working title. Does the title you've chosen market your film well?

In my classes, I ask people to give feedback to each other regarding all the aspects of the writing. For instance, students bring a synopsis to class. They read each other's synopsis and answer a series of questions. The first set of questions is about the title. "Was the title intriguing?" "What did it mean to you?" "Would it prompt you to go see the movie?"

I use TCA as an example and model receiving feedback before they give each other feedback. The answers I usually get from students to the title questions are:

"The affair implies both a romantic encounter and a dramatic situation."

"It reminded me of *The Thomas Crown Affair*."

"I like it."

"It's intriguing."

On one occasion, a student said, "It doesn't mean anything to me…." That was a first. I'm standing in front of a classroom filled with people. What am I going to say?

I held up a handout which lists the ground rules for giving feedback. One of the rules states: If you want to help someone improve… you must provide an Alternative Positive Behavior. Then I asked, "What would you name my film?"

Her response was so good, I decided to rename *The Tranby Croft Affair*. It's now called *A Deadly Sketch*.

Your title should tell the prospective viewers enough to get them to the theatre. Furthermore, I am still open to an even better title.

Your Turn

Complete the following exercise:

Analyze your script and rewrite scenes as necessary for:
- Raising the Level of Antagonism
- Adding Some Secrets or Twists
- Improving Character Dimension
- Ensuring a Character Arc
- Using Imagery
- Getting the Title Right

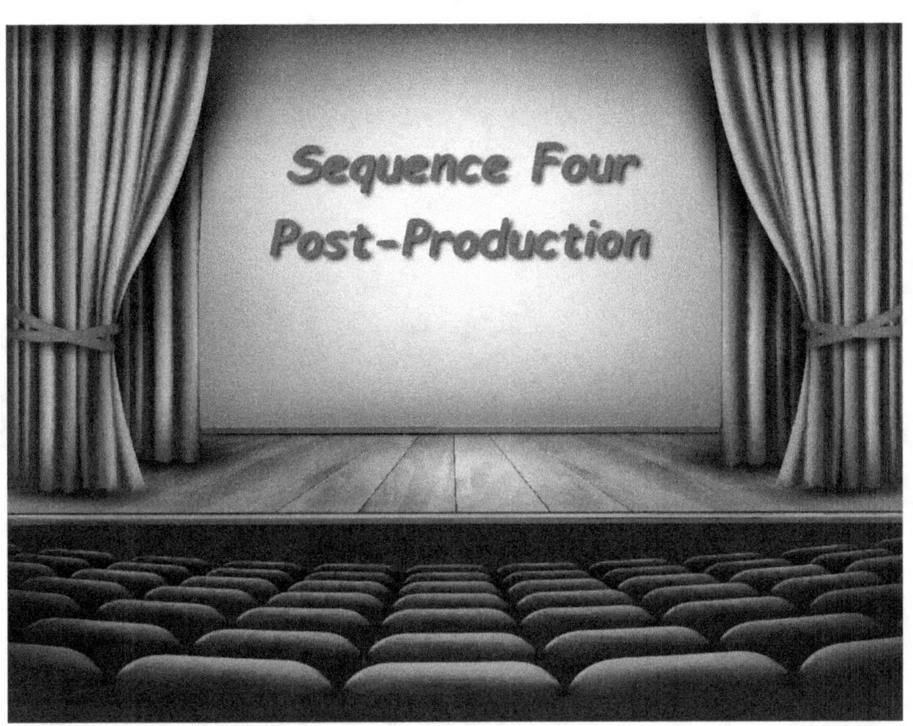
Sequence Four
Post-Production

Scene 10

Sell is Not a 4-Letter Word

I think they should consider giving Oscars for meetings: Best
Meeting of the Year, Best Supporting Meeting, Best Meeting
Based on Material from Another Meeting.

> – William Goldman *Adventures in the Screen Trade*

Marketing Tips

You've finished the script and now what? It's time to start the hard work…selling it. Here are some tips for selling your script:

Document Your Authorship

Although I've advised you to rewrite your script, it is wise to send your first draft to the Writer's Guild of America west as soon as you finish it. This will serve as proof of the completion date and virtual copyright in case of a lawsuit later. Visit the website www.wga.org for instructions. Scroll to the bottom of the home page and click "Register Your Script."

The process is quite easy. If there are co-writers, you'll need the Social Security Number or Driver's License for each. After completing the registration form, you'll pay \$20 per script, and upload a .pdf of the script, and voila, you're done.

You may also want to mail a hard copy of the script to yourself via the United States Postal Service. Some people suggest sending it registered mail which requires that you sign a receipt that it was delivered to you. Sounds like overkill to me. The main reason you are mailing it to yourself is to show the post mark on the envelope. DON'T open the envelope. If you sue someone for stealing your material, the origination date will be the issue. You will take the envelope to court, enter it into evidence, and let the court open it. This is sometimes referred to as "poor man's copyright."

Assuming you have rewritten the script consistent with the information in the previous chapters, you may want to register it again, especially if the title has changed, there are significant plot changes, new characters, etc.

Marketing Essentials

As you approach Producers, Agents, Managers, or anyone else in the industry that might influence a sale, you'll need several documents:

- A 30-second pitch
- A more in-depth pitch
- A query letter (see Scene 11)
- A synopsis (see Scene 12)
- A treatment (see Scene 13)
- The script (see Scene 14)

Never send a script to anyone unsolicited. You first need to contact your prospect and seek an advance. An advance isn't money up front. In sales terminology, it means to move the sales cycle to the next level. Let's say you telephone Mr. Producer and you deliver your 30-second pitch. He says, "Tell me more," which from your point of view is an advance. You've got some interest. So, you deliver your more in-depth pitch. He says, "Send me something." "Something" could be a synopsis, a treatment, or the script. Ideally, he'll want the script, but if he says synopsis or treatment, ask, "How many pages would you like to see?" A synopsis can be from 2 – 4 pages, while a treatment is usually 6 – 10 pages.

Perfecting the Pitch

The 30-second pitch is like the logline only less formal because it's spoken, not read. A logline is one sentence which describes the Protagonist, Antagonist, genre, setting, and story essence. If you call a production company and the person asks, "What's your story about?" You might say something like this:

> *It's about a Crime Illustrator in San Francisco who sketches an exact likeness of a murder suspect. When the drawing airs on the eleven o'clock news, the murderer sees it, and begins stalking the artist. It's called*

> – A Deadly Sketch

The best way to find examples of pitches may be to search YouTube for "How to Pitch Your Screenplay." You'll find a plethora of examples. You will also see sites where you can post your pitch for producers to see; such as, www.moviepitch.com and http://virtualpitchfest.com

You'll also need a more in-depth pitch for when your prospect says, "Tell me more." I like using the seven plot elements from Scene 1 the Getting Started chapter, but this should be more conversational because you are speaking to a person. You don't want to sound automated. For *A Deadly Sketch*, it might sound like this:

Well, my Crime Illustrator, Tranby Croft, works for the San Francisco Police Department and provides drawings for a segment called Bay-Tips on the local news.

On the 4th of July, a wealthy Japanese businessman is murdered outside the backdoor of the Otafuku Tei restaurant. A team of detectives led by Mitchell Fields investigates and determines the victim is a Yakuza mob boss.

Fields asks Tranby to draw a composite from an eyewitness account of the murder. Turns out it was an exact likeness of the murderer. When it appears on the Bay-Tips show, the murderer phones Tranby and threatens to kill her.

A mystery writer named Harris Richardson approaches Tranby to get ideas from her perspective that he might use in his next novel. But when the suspect begins stalking Tranby, Harris tries to protect her by insisting she go into hiding, which she does because she is falling in love with him.

The syndicate's top bosses vow to avenge their fallen leader.

Meanwhile, Tranby starts to suspect the news anchor on the Bay-Tips show is involved and develops a creative plan to uncover her. The police start to suspect that Harris is involved in some way and they arrest him for obstruction of justice.

When Harris is released from jail, the murderer follows him to Tranby's hiding place. It looks like all is lost, when...Tranby mortally wounds the murderer just before the police arrive.

A twist in the tale occurs when the murderer, in his dying breath, reveals the identity of the real culprit. The man who hired him to make the hit.

In the end, Tranby goes back to work, Harris publishes his novel appropriately entitled, "The Tranby Croft Affair," and they discuss working together in the future.

Here is another Deadly Sketch pitch applying Michael Hauge's template from *Selling Your Story in 60 Seconds*. He does warn that you need to read his entire book for this to make sense. So, buy it and read it. It's great. Now when the listener says, "Tell me more." You say:

Let me begin by telling you how I came up with this story idea. I was reading a copy of Los Angeles magazine and they have a regular piece called, A Day in the Life. It features an interview with someone who has a unique job. This specific article was about a Crime Illustrator who did courtroom illustration and crime scene re-enactments for Eyewitness News.

I started thinking, "What if a sketch artist draws a likeness of a murderer and then the murderer threatens her?" And that's how I came up with the idea for A Deadly Sketch, a story about a naive 28-year old woman who works as a Crime Illustrator for the San Francisco Police Department and provides drawings for a segment called Bay-Tips on the local news.

Then, she draws a composite from an eyewitness account of a murder. Turns out to be an exact likeness of the murderer. The night it appears on the Bay-Tips show, she receives a chilling phone call from the murder suspect.

But when her new love interest is arrested for the crime, she must learn to use her creativity to solve the mystery herself before the real culprit catches up with her. Ultimately, she must defeat the vengeful adversary.

Once you have honed the pitch as well as you can, you must rehearse, rehearse, rehearse, until it becomes natural.

You'll also need a creative query letter, a synopsis, treatment, and the final draft of the script ready to go. Samples can be found in Scenes 11, 12, 13, and 14 respectively. Now, let's move on to the marketing plan.

Marketing Plan

The purpose of a marketing plan is to sell your script or get a writing assignment. First, you'll need to do some research to determine who will buy your type of script and isolate individuals to contact.

Resources

Here are four resources every screenwriter should have:

1.   *Variety* is the preeminent entertainment industry source for who's doing what in Hollywood.

2.   *Scr(i)pt* magazine will keep you abreast of the technical aspects of the craft.

3.   *Writer's Market* not only provides listings of agents and publishers, it provides tutorials on query letter writing, pitching, contracts, bookkeeping and pricing, and play and screenwriting contests.

4.   *Hollywood Screenwriting Directory* provides the contact information for over 4000 industry insiders. Check it out at the Writer's Store https://www.writersstore.com/hollywood-screenwriting-directory/.

Prepare Your Written Plan

Selling yourself is a numbers game. The more people you contact, the higher your probability of success.

The first step is to determine whom you are going to contact. Make a list of prospects who have produced the kind of film you've written. Whether it be feature film, TV series, cable movie, etc.

Find their numbers and start calling. If you get voice mail, leave a slightly expanded version of your pitch plus your call-back information. Best times to call are early morning (7:30 – 8:30) or late afternoon (5:00 – 6:00). At these times, you're less likely to get the gate-keeper, but don't limit your calling to only two hours a day.

When you talk on the phone, your goal is to get an advance. In priority:

1.   Face-to-face meeting

2.   Sending information

Face-to-face increases your odds. There is a 10% chance of being hired from written information. There is a 33% chance when you meet the buyer face-to-face.

If you are asked to send written information, go for the full script first. If the prospect asks for a synopsis, reply, "I have the script completed. I'd be happy to send it straight away." Or something to that effect.

I also recommend you keep an activity log. Write down the contact's name, company name, the date and time of the contact, how you contacted (phone, e-mail, face-to-face, query letter), comments (not interested, asked for submission, etc.), and note when to follow-up.

Marketing Strategy

You may want to find an agent first, but there is a catch-22 in Hollywood. The adage is, "You can't get an agent until you've sold a script and you can't sell a script without an agent."

I read an article in Writer's Digest magazine many years ago. It was about Cynthia Whitcomb who wrote 10 scripts in 3 years in different genres to find out which one she liked the most and to see where she might fit in the Hollywood scene. She then sent 12 copies of each script to various producers and directors of the applicable genre. Tony Bill contacted her about one of the scripts and asked her to reset the story in a different time. She refused, but he later hired her to write the screen story for something he already owned. Moral of the story, if a producer asks, "Do you have anything else?" You need to have 3 to 10 pitches ready to go.

For example, here are mine:

1. Sci-Fi – *The Pan-Horus Project 3013* - When a doomed Earth is evacuated to an Eden-esque replacement, the brilliant architect of humanity's hope uncovers a nefarious plot to enslave the colonists and must fight a tyrant to save his family and mankind.

2. Disney Style Family Comedy – *Vermont Family Cyclers* - What happens when an innkeeper sells out his place to a group of Bikers.

3. Western – *One Riot One Ranger* - What if the legend were true? One Texas Ranger, just one man is sent to handle a riot in the Texas Hill Country.

4. Love Story – *Seasons of Life* - A thirty-something Trainer challenges his present life structure and destroys what he has built in his twenties for a Twenty-something Administrator who is trying to create her own dream and find a mentor.

5. Wacky Comedy – *The Warren Missile Crisis* - What happens when a small town is divided by the fate of a rusting Redstone missile, erected in Town Square 20 years earlier as a tribute to the VFW.

6.   Drug-running – *Impulse Decision* - What does a rental car employee do when he finds six million dollars in the trunk of a returned vehicle and discovers it was stolen from drug-runners?

7.   Murder Mystery – *A Deadly Sketch* - A Crime Illustrator is propelled into a race for her life when she sketches an exact likeness of a murder suspect and becomes his object of pursuit.

8.   Thriller – *False Pretense* - A Pediatrician diagnoses a healthy child with a rare immune deficiency; so, he can conduct experiments in isolation and publish his findings to meet his residency requirements.

9.   Sports Story – *The Second Decade* - A boy's dreams are crushed when he's cut from the St. Louis Cardinals rookie league team.

10. Con Artist – *Revenge Syndrome* - The Sting meets The Da Vinci Code.

The scripts have been completed for six of these. Two have outlines finished. The other two are in the embryonic stage. I would only pitch ones that have been completed. But might also say to my prospect, "I have a few other ideas that I could send to you once they're more developed."

Now, I like this strategy, particularly, if you haven't decided on your niche. It's a great learning experience and provides opportunity for practice writing in different styles, as well as, marketing to different audiences.

On the other hand, some would say you should focus on becoming the best you can be in one specific genre. The argument is, if I'm a producer looking for a thriller; I'm looking for the best thriller writer available.

Implement the Plan

Okay, get out there and start prospecting. Contact as many people as you can. Make friends with low-level assistants. They can get your property read. Don't forget local production companies. You might want to check out InkTip – http://www.inktip.com and Spec Scout – https://www.specscout.com

There are many contests you might choose to enter. My favorite is the Austin Film Festival - www.austinfilmfestival.com. Here are two other websites to check out: Screen Craft – http://www.screencraft.org and Without a Box - www.withoutabox.com.

If you place in a contest, make sure you add that to your query letter.

Write Your Acceptance Speech

You might think this is presumptuous, but there is a method to my madness. When I watch the Academy Awards Show it bothers me how horrible the speeches are, especially when an actor pulls out a folded sheet of paper and reads it or says, "I'd like to thank so and so." These people are professional actors; they can't act an acceptance speech?

Here is an example of what to say. Practice it. Rehearse it until it becomes as natural as your pitch. Repeat after me, "My heartfelt thanks goes out to Don Simonds for teaching me everything I know about screenwriting." That's a long "I" in my last name. It's not Simmons, it's pronounced Sigh -mons.

But seriously, the purpose of writing your acceptance speech is about self-image psychology. I believe you should prepare affirmations for all the goals you have.

Attitudes are based upon your belief system; the assumptions, concepts, values, and practices that constitute the way you view reality. If you believe you can't do something, you won't even try. It's impossible to bring about meaningful change if you do nothing.

The key to controlling your attitude is to control your self-talk. What you think is critical, what you affirm will happen. Here are some guidelines for creating your affirmations:

1. They need to be personal – Affirm what is right for you. Write each as an "I" statement.
2. Always use positive language – Describe the positive result not what you are trying to correct.
3. State them in present tense – Assume the change has happened already, not "someday."
4. Describe achievement of the goal or habit – Write "I am" or "I have" not "I will."
5. Avoid comparisons – Affirm what is right for you not "I'm as good as William Goldman."
6. Use action words – "I enjoy," "I love to," "I show," "I feel," etc.
7. Use excitement words – Use words that spark an emotional picture like "I happily."
8. Be truthful – Affirm what you can honestly imagine yourself becoming.
9. Balance – Strive for growth in all areas of your life.
10. Realistic – Perfection is self-defeating. Avoid "I always," or "I'll never."
11. Private – Your affirmations are for your eyes only.

Examples:

I am an action person. I do first things first and one thing at a time.

It's fun and easy to write and rewrite scenes.

I have a positive expectancy of reaching my goals and I vividly know my plan of attack.

My life is filled with interesting story ideas.

I am logical and quick in making important plot, character or dialogue decisions.

I am Pygmalion to myself and to all my characters.

I don't have to do anything. I want to, I choose to, I like it, It's my idea.

I easily keep up-to-date on industry trends.

Guidelines for Imprinting

A.   Read the affirmation

B.   Picture the end result

C.   Feel the emotion of accomplishment

Repeat the process at least twice each day.

Your Turn

Complete the following exercises:

1.   Register your script with WGA.
2.   Prepare your marketing plan.
3.   Write the Synopsis, Treatment, Pitches, Query Letter, etc.
4.   Prepare and rehearse your 1 – 3-minute pitch.
5.   Finish polishing the marketing draft.
6.   Implement your marketing plan.
7.   Write your Academy Award acceptance speech.

Scene 11

Query Letters

Every Sale Has a Story! ... how are you going to get that story sold to the people on your list? Well:

> *In person* is better than a phone call…
> *A phone call* is better than a query letter…
> *A query letter* is better than an e-mail…
> And *an e-mail* (from a stranger) is usually when I push the DELETE on my computer.…

– Blake Snyder Save the Cat

Query Letters

There are many different formats but basically the query letter should include a description of the story and the author's credentials.

The first example shows my letter for A DEADLY SKETCH. Notice there is no chitchat. I jump right into the story synopsis, followed by my credentials, and offer my services on assignment as well.

The second example is from a group project. Notice the heading shows a return address from The Pan-Horus Group. I started the letter with information about our group, included the logline, and the next to the last paragraph mentions our placement in the writing competition. Finally, I have listed all four writers in the salutation.

Following are the two examples I referred to above:

DONALD E. SIMONDS

1528 Query Letter Circle

Plano, Texas 75075

555.282.6517

scriptwriter@sbcglobal.net

Dear Mr. Producer:

Crime Illustrator, Tranby Croft, works for the San Francisco Police Department and provides drawings for a segment called *Bay Tips* on a local news station. *Bay Tips* displays crime scene or reenactment drawings and offers rewards for information leading to an arrest.

Tranby draws an extraordinary likeness of a murder suspect from an eye witness account, which airs on *Bay Tips*. The murderer sees the report and begins stalking Tranby. Consequently, she is propelled into a race for her life.

A DEADLY SKETCH is a suspense story with a strong female protagonist that builds to an ingenious ending. It is a story of injustice, obstruction of justice, and how creativity can solve even life-threatening problems.

During the bulk of my career, I have produced more than 20 training films and have performed the duties of Writer, Director, Actor, and Crew. Furthermore, I've set the strategic vision as the Producer for most of them. One is a Telly award winner.

I have a variety of theatrical scripts and story ideas, but I'm also interested in assignments. I look forward to hearing from you soon.

Sincerely,

Donald E. Simonds

The Pan-Horus Group
1528 Query Letter Circle
Plano, Texas 75075
555.282.6517
thepanhorusgroup@sbcglobal.net

Dear Mr. Producer:

Our team, with experience in writing novels, documentaries, and producing training films, as well as performing the roles of writer, art director, and actor on various film projects, has collectively written a feature screenplay, which we would like to submit to you.

The logline for the film is:

When a doomed Earth is evacuated to an Eden-esque replacement, the brilliant architect of humanity's hope uncovers a nefarious plot to enslave the colonists and must fight a tyrant to save his family and mankind.

"The Pan-Horus Project 3013" is a sci-fi mystery similar to films like "Elysium" and "Oblivion."

In the year 3013, The Global Space Administration reports that Earth has left its orbit, threatening mankind with extinction. The Department of Space Immigration orders the immediate evacuation of Earth to the planet Pan-Horus where brilliant, young architect Noah Lambson has designed colossal 500-story housing units for man's salvation. But, Noah discovers that the General in charge of humanity's relocation has a sinister plot planned for the colonist. To save the lives of his family and the next arrival of colonists, Noah must stop the General.

"The Pan-Horus Project 3013" reached the semi-finals of the 2016 Final Draft Big Break Competition. It will appeal to a wide audience of science fiction fans. The film deals with themes of extinction, tyranny, and hope.

We appreciate your time and consideration. Please let me know if I may send you the completed script.

Sincerely,

Isabella Garza
Christy-Ann Hamlin
Mark Majeski
Donald E. Simonds

Scene 12

Synopsis

I've been reading (and I used to write) synopses and treatments my entire career, and I have yet to encounter one that's emotionally involving.

— Michael Hauge *Selling Your Story in 60 Seconds*

Synopsis

A synopsis is usually between two and four pages, although it depends upon whom is making the request. For instance, if you submit online through InkTip or some similar website, you'll be asked to limit your synopsis to 450 words. Furthermore, you may be asked to submit a four-sentence synopsis.

The key as Michael Hauge alludes to above is how to make it engaging? It needs to be powerful. You should get feedback on it and polish it until it conveys the story as effectively as possible. Take copies with you to meetings, but leave it behind only if you cannot get the buyer to read the whole script.

Here is the final synopsis of A DEADLY SKETCH, plus two condensed versions:

SYNOPSIS

"A DEADLY SKETCH"
by
Donald E. Simonds

Crime Illustrator, Tranby Croft, works for the San Francisco Police Department and provides drawings for a segment called *Bay Tips* on the local TV station. *Bay Tips* shows crime scene details or reenactments and offers rewards for information leading to arrests in hopes that citizens will call with information. The host of the show is a stereotypical news anchor named Melinda Gary.

On the 4th of July, a wealthy Japanese businessman is murdered outside the backdoor of the Otafuku Tei restaurant. Ross, a member of Detective Mitchell Fields' team suggests that the victim is a Yakuza mob boss.

Fields asks Tranby to draw a composite from an eye witness account and she creates an extraordinarily accurate likeness of the murderer. The sketch airs during the eleven o'clock *Bay Tips* show, during which Tranby's name is inadvertently mentioned.

The murderer sees the report, calls, and threatens Tranby.

Harris Richardson, a mystery writer, also sees the report and approaches Tranby with a proposal to work together on a novel based upon some of her exploits. She reluctantly accepts his offer.

More murders occur and *Bay Tips* airs the image of the suspect again. The suspect begins stalking Tranby, which propels her into a race for her life as he makes her the object of his pursuit.

Romantic sparks fly between Harris and Tranby and, in his misguided zeal; he tries to protect Tranby by insisting she go into hiding. The police begin to suspect Harris is the murderer and Mitchell Fields advises Tranby to stay away from Harris. But alas, she follows her heart.

The syndicate's top bosses meet at the victim's mansion on Tiburon to discuss who will be his successor as the Godfather. The victim's wife speaks to the board of directors to explain that her husband left explicit instructions that they should exact revenge for her husband's death before a new Godfather is elected.

Meanwhile, Mitchell and his team's investigators uncover prime suspect, Martin Mayhew.

Harris and Tranby consummate their relationship. Later that night Harris spots Martin, recognizes him from Tranby's drawing, and chases him through Nob Hill, but Martin eludes Harris. A confrontation between Harris and Detective Fields leads to Harris' arrest for obstruction of justice.

Tranby becomes suspicious of Melinda Gary's use of her name on the air and devises an ingenious plan to trick her into disclosing what she knows about the perpetrator.

Ross takes it upon himself to go to a Yakuza gambling house and witnesses a Yubitsume (pinkie extraction).

When Harris is released from jail, Martin follows him to Tranby's hiding place.

Consequently, Martin and his sidekick get to Tranby, but detective Fields arrives and he, Harris, and Tranby prevail.

A twist in the tale occurs when Martin's dying breath reveals that one of the syndicate generals put a contract out on the Godfather so he could take over.

After all the suspects are arrested, Tranby goes back to work, Harris publishes his novel, entitled appropriately, "The Tranby Croft Affair," and they consider future collaborations.

Synopsis not to exceed 450 words

Crime Illustrator, Tranby Croft, works for the San Francisco Police Department and provides drawings for Bay-Tips on the local TV station. Bay-Tips shows crime scene details or reenactments and offers rewards for information leading to arrests. The host of the show is a stereotypical news anchor named Melinda Gary.

On the 4th of July, a wealthy Japanese businessman is murdered outside the backdoor of the Otafuku Tei restaurant. Ross, a member of Detective Mitchell Fields' team suggests that the victim is a Yakuza mob boss.

Tranby draws a composite from an eyewitness account, an extraordinarily accurate likeness of the murderer. The sketch airs during the eleven o'clock Bay-Tips show, during which Tranby's name is inadvertently mentioned. The murderer sees the report, calls and threatens Tranby.

Harris Richardson, a mystery writer, also sees the report and approaches Tranby with a proposal to work together on a novel based upon some of her exploits. She reluctantly accepts his offer.

More murders occur and Bay-Tips airs the image of the suspect again. The suspect begins stalking Tranby, which propels her into a race for her life as he makes her the object of his pursuit.

Romantic sparks fly between Harris and Tranby and he tries to protect Tranby by hiding her. The police begin to suspect Harris is the murderer and Mitchell Fields advises Tranby to stay away from Harris. But alas, she follows her heart.

The syndicate's top bosses meet at the victim's mansion in Tiburon to discuss who will be his successor as the Godfather. The victim's wife speaks to the board of directors to explain that her husband left explicit instructions that they should exact revenge for her his death before a new Godfather is elected.

Meanwhile, Mitchell and his team uncover prime suspect, Martin Mayhew.

Late one night, Harris spots Martin driving past Tranby's apartment and chases him through Nob Hill but Martin escapes. Detective Fields arrests Harris for obstruction of justice.

Tranby becomes suspicious of Melinda Gary's use of her name on the air and devises an ingenious plan to trick her into disclosing what she knows about the perpetrator.

Ross takes it upon himself to go to a Yakuza gambling house and witnesses a Yubitsume (pinkie extraction).

When Harris is released from jail, Martin follows him to Tranby's hiding place. Martin gets to Tranby but she fatally wounds him.

Martin's dying breath reveals that one of the syndicate generals put a contract out on the Godfather so he could take over.

After all the suspects are arrested, Tranby goes back to work, Harris publishes his novel, entitled appropriately, "The Tranby Croft Affair," and they consider future collaborations.

Four Lines Only

- Crime Illustrator, Tranby Croft, draws crime scene reenactments for a local TV station.
- A murder suspect stalks her after he sees an exact likeness of himself that she drew.
- While running for her life, Tranby develops an ingenious plan to solve the crime.
- The murderer finds Tranby's hideout and all appears lost when... Tranby fatally wounds the suspect.

Scene 13

Treatment

If you are required to write out the complete story, I suggest that you write three to ten pages covering your plot. Your style needn't be anything fancier than a sixth grade book report. The emphasis here is to ensure that everyone at all levels will "get" the story.

> – Robert Kosberg *How to Sell Your Idea to Hollywood*

Treatment

Treatments are usually between six and ten pages long. However, they may be longer. The treatment for Aliens was 45 pages. Some executives may ask for a treatment of twenty or more pages.

The structure of the treatment can be more like a short story than a script, but should still be written in present tense. Focus on the narrative and avoid things like scene headings which can distract the reader.

In the past, writers have pitched story ideas using a treatment before writing the full script. Now, Spec Scripts are seldom sold before written.

Also, you may choose to write a Treatment between the scene card step and the first draft. This added effort seems redundant to me; however, some may find it useful in flushing out the story components.

I write the script and use the most important scenes to construct the Treatment as a marketing tool for my finished script.

Here is the Treatment for A DEADLY SKETCH:

"A DEADLY SKETCH"

TREATMENT
By
Donald E. Simonds

Fog partially covers the Golden Gate Bridge. The fog moves
fast toward the San Francisco skyline.

As darkness falls, crowds stroll onto the Golden Gate bridge.

The fog lifts enough for literally thousands of spectators to
see three fireboats as they start spraying rainbow colored
streams of water from all seven nozzles. The crowd cheers
the traditional fourth of July celebration as San Francisco's
finest turns the show into a colorful water ballet.

The lights of Japan Center shine bright and the streets fill
with more people moving about.

A man, MARTIN, 45, moves slowly in the shadows near the
Pagoda.

His mouth opens slightly, his breath visible in the cool
night air. He moves on an apparently aimless course. He
looks average; average build, average height, average
everything.

The back door to a Japanese restaurant swings open and a tiny
man, MARIKU YAMASHIRA, 60, steps out. A tiny woman, MRS.
YAMASHIRA, 55, follows. They wear dinner attire; he in a
suit, she in a cocktail dress.

He weaves like a drunk and she says so. They start chattering
in Japanese. The woman leaves.

Martin comes out of the shadows. He pulls a .45 caliber
handgun from his waistband, aims at Yamashira, and pulls the
trigger.

When the shell hits Mariku Yamashira there is no initial
pain. He looks surprised from the pressure. He reaches for
his chest. He realizes that he has been hit. Martin fires
another shot which hits Yamashira in the head. It explodes
blood all over the wall and forces him into a garbage pile.

He dies, eyes open, lifeless.

DETECTIVE MITCHELL FIELDS sits at his desk, drinking coffee
and looking at the mounds of paperwork which he faces for the
day.

                    Screenwriting Fundamentals

He looks like a cowboy, an old Texas Ranger with gray hair. His face, weathered from years of police work, appears older than his 50 years.

Through the radio, Fields hears a Patrolman's voice, "...Send homicide, forensic, and an ambulance to the Buchanan Mall... We've got a body at the back door of Otafuku Tei, the restaurant directly across from the Japan Center Pagoda."

Two homicide detectives hover at the outer edge of the forensic team, ROSS and MCNALLY. Ross, 32, listens to one of the ambulance attendants while McNally, 45, gracefully sidesteps a police photographer and sketches the crime scene on a clipboard pad. One of the forensic men measures, with a long tape, the distance from the body to the street; the body to the wall; the body to the back door of the restaurant. Two other members of the team poke around in the garbage for evidence.

McNally refers to his note pad. The victim's name is Mariku Yamashira. He was a very wealthy businessman.

Crime Illustrator TRANBY CROFT, 28, sits in the front row of a courtroom gallery. She looks like a fashion model, very attractive, feminine, shapely with an athletic body. Her dark brown hair accentuates her face. Her eyes, translucent teal, the most unique shade imaginable, mesmerize.

She sketches scenarios for the evening news. It's about 10:00 A.M. The prosecutor makes his opening remarks.

Using Design Markers, she draws a scene with the Judge in the middle and the Prosecutor to the left and the Jury on the right. The Defense Attorney and the Defendant sit farthest from the Jury and, although the Prosecutor faces the jury box, he points at the accused.

The Defense Attorney's voice drops to barely audible. Tranby draws a likeness of the Defendant. She takes her eyes off the sketch pad to look at him for very brief moments. Then her eyes move quickly back to the pad. Her body does not move except for her right arm as she rapidly captures this man's image.

He turns slightly toward her and smiles a Charles Manson smile.

Detectives Fields, Ross, and McNally enter the autopsy room. BYERS, late 40's, bald, beer gut, meets them at the door. Without a word, Byers leads the detectives to the table occupied by Mariku Yamashira.

The tiny man lays naked, but from a distance appears to be fully clothed. The closer they get the easier it is to determine that Yamashira sports a full body tattoo.

The neckline starts just under his collarbone, extends down his arms to the elbows, covers his complete torso, and ends at his knees.

Although his genitals remain flesh tone, they blend into the scene, almost unnoticeable. With delight, Ross declares he is Yakuza! An insignia tattooed over the dead man's heart appears to be a medallion. The gang's badge of membership.

Tranby meets with Mrs. Lee, an eye witness, alone in a vacant office. Tranby starts to make sketches.

Tranby asks Mrs. Lee about basic head shape. The face starts to appear. They sit side-by-side Tranby adds hair to the sketch. Tranby tacks the drawing to the wall and they examine it. Finally, Mrs. Lee approves the sketch.

The Yamashira mansion perches like a monument to wealth on the Tiburon coast.

Looking out the great room window, one can see the panorama of San Francisco Bay from Emeryville to the Golden Gate Bridge and everything in between.

At 7 p.m. the procession of Oyabun, the top Yakuza bosses, streams into the great room. All thin and short, wear the same shiny suits with a lapel pin that matches the tattoo on Yamashira's chest.

Each of the twelve members of the Board of Directors places a tribute in an ornate bowl, positioned at the entrance to the great room.

All the men sit in the lavish living-room furniture. Mrs. Yamashira stands at the hearth. She explains the purpose of the meeting is to decide what to do about the murderer and to begin the selection process for a successor.

Each board member opens an envelope and withdraws a single sheet of paper. She reads from the instruction sheet.

Here are the rules: One; No lobbying for votes. Two; no election until after burial, no election until we have concluded our business with his murderer. Three; each board member will name the individual who best represents the values of giri-ninjo of obligation and compassion, and several characteristics of an exceptional leader. Four; a two-thirds majority vote is required, and she will lead the voting process, when the time comes.

Everyone nods agreement.

They look at the characteristics to consider, listed on the back of this paper. Everyone turns the page over as she continues. These are listed in order of importance to the job. They are: obligation and compassion, judgment,

operational planning, leadership and influence, and
compatibility of personal values with the values of the
organization. She asks for any questions?

Silence, Mrs. Yamashira adjourns the meeting. Each board
member approaches her to convey his sympathy for her loss,
then departs.

HARRIS RICHARDSON, 32, suave and debonair, could have been a
basketball player, sits in front of his television watching
the eleven o'clock news.

MELINDA GARY, 38, stereotypical news anchor, gives her
report. She explains that Crime Illustrator, Tranby Croft,
has developed a sketch based upon an eye witness account.

The drawing fills the screen. Melinda suggests if anyone
should see the man, please call BayTips...

The letters BayTips are SUPERIMPOSED on the T.V. screen.
Under each letter is the corresponding number, 229-8477.

Harris watches the report. Harris lives with his sister. He
asks her to come watch the report with him.

SUSAN, 30, tall like Harris, might have been a runner-up in
the Miss California contest several years earlier, would have
undoubtedly won the swimsuit competition, enters the room.

Harris tells Susan he's going to have to meet this Tranby
Croft.

Tranby bends over the art table within her apartment
developing some drawings for the BayTips show. The intercom
buzzes. She presses the speaker button.

Harris Richardson stands at the front door holding a handset
to his ear. Tranby's voice comes through the speaker.

Harris fidgets nervously, waits for Tranby to decide whether
to let him in or not. Finally, she tells Harris to meet her
across the street at a coffee shop.

When Tranby approaches Harris inside the coffee shop, he
pauses and tries not to smile like men do when lust destroys
their brains. His eyes sparkle as he gazes upon Tranby Croft
for the first time. The object of his most passionate
desires stands before him.

Later that night, she hops into bed, slips under the sheets.
Tranby lays there for a few moments contemplating what might
happen between her and Harris. She smiles a warm cuddly kind
of smile and rolls over. She reaches for the light and turns
it off. The room darkens. Some street noise filters into her
room, but otherwise everything is still.

She breathes deeply, her eyes move beneath the lids, indicating a dream state. The serenity is broken by the loud sound of the telephone ringing. It startles her. She sits up abruptly and answers the phone. The murderer says, "If I see my face on Channel 2 again, you're dead...Understand? Dead." The phone clicks, followed by a dial tone.

Fields rings the doorbell at the Yamashira mansion. A servant answers the door. Fields hands her his card. The woman invites him in and escorts him to the great room.

The servant encourages him to take a seat then leaves. A few moments later, Mrs. Yamashira enters the room.

Fields asks her what kind of work her husband was in?

She explains in the Japanese culture, women are subservient, eager to obey. She would not presume to ask about her husband's business.

Fields asks about the full body tattoo.

She explains the custom of body art to ward off evil spirits, to bring luck to the family, and to test his mettle.

Fields reaches into a file folder and withdraws the close-up of the insignia on Yamashira's chest. He hands the photograph to her. He asks what it represents?

She explains the Yakuza are a necessary vice for Japanese society. They were underdog folk heroes who stood up for the poor and the defenseless, like the Anglo-American myth of Robin Hood.

Tranby and Harris examine her apartment door. The lock is scratched and obviously burgled. Harris dials 911. Moments later a patrol car pulls up in front of the building.

AARON BANKS, 30, Martin's wheel man stands at Tranby's front window, tells Martin the cops have arrived. Martin crushes a cigarette into an ashtray and leads Aaron out the back door and down the fire escape.

Two patrol officers pull their weapons and enter the apartment. No one is in the apartment. However, they do find the cigarette. Evidence someone was there.

TAKAYAMA, 55, one of the syndicate bosses, speaks to the council in the great room at the Yamashira mansion. He tells the group that he knows Martin Mayhew. The Yakuza took control of his construction company, sold off the assets, and took the profit from him. He would have every reason to want to retaliate.

The Directors establish a plan to get Martin and adjourn.

Fields and Ross go on stakeout to a restaurant supply warehouse. They see Martin enter the warehouse and follow. Before they can get across the street, the warehouse explodes. No bodies found in the debris.

The next day, Fields interviews Takayama, who denies knowing who Martin is. Takayama also lauds Yamashira as a great man.

Harris convinces Tranby to go into hiding until the murderer is apprehended. He drives them to an art gallery in Sausalito.

DENNIS JOHNSON, 35, opens the alley door as Harris, Susan and Tranby enter. Dennis offers a guest bedroom to Tranby for as long as she needs it.

There is a bed in the loft, a small dresser, some other small furniture, nothing fancy... the way a man would decorate. As Harris enters the room, Tranby looks out a large picture window toward San Francisco Bay. Harris approaches her from behind.

They embrace and kiss passionately. She unbuttons his shirt. He helps her from her clothes. They tumble to the sheets. Skin to skin, she's on top. We hear the sounds of love making. After a few minutes, they roll over and Harris takes the top position. Background music comes from downstairs, something like, "Take my breath away," by Berlin.

The couple make love for quite some time and when they finish, they breathe heavily and appear worn out.

They cuddle together.

Martin and Aaron drive past the front of Tranby's building, heading west on Sacramento Street. By now there are police cars double parked in front of the building. Fields and Ross talk to one another near the stoop.

The two criminals discuss the matter. This place is crawling with cops. They have to get out of there.

Harris' car turns the corner.

Martin looks straight at Harris.

Harris sees Martin and obviously recognizes his face from the BayTips broadcast.

Aaron slams down the accelerator. His car jumps out ahead of Harris' car. The chase is on, as Harris hits his accelerator.

Both cars weave in and out of traffic through the streets of San Francisco, culminating at Filbert street.

Just past Hyde Street, Filbert, drops at about a forty-five-degree angle toward Leavenworth. Aaron takes the jump at fifty miles per hour.

Harris speeds toward the jump point, hoping that Aaron will chicken out. He doesn't. Aaron's car sails through the air. About 100 feet down from the pinnacle, Aaron's car smashes to the pavement.

Harris slams on the brakes. Harris' car goes into a slide and comes to a stop.

The right tires of Harris' car perch precariously on the edge of the cliff. He jumps from the driver's side out into the street and runs to the back of the car. Looking east on Filbert, Harris sees Aaron's car turn left on Jones street heading toward Fisherman's Wharf.

Harris goes back to Tranby's apartment to report the sighting, but, Ross takes Harris to a patrol car, handcuffs him and puts him in the car. He's under arrest for obstruction of Justice.

Meanwhile, the Yamashira family conduct a traditional Japanese funeral. Thousands attend.

The attendant at the crematorium gives the two Generals the urn and chopsticks for the entire family. The attendant opens the casket and the family members pick bones out of the ashes and place them in the urn.

Fields, Ross, and McNally drive across the Bay Bridge toward Oakland. Fields knocks on Martin Mayhew's door. No answer. He rings the doorbell. No answer.

A neighbor woman approaches Fields and explains that after the second BayTips broadcast, she saw Martin load his car with a suitcase and drive away. He hasn't been back since.

Melinda Gary walks past the crew and toward Chris Williams' office. As she gets to the desk just outside the office door, Chris' phone rings. Melinda looks around to see where the secretary is. Locating no one, she picks up the receiver.

Tranby tells Melinda she has a plan to get the guy who is murdering all the people. She'll be sending Melinda some drawings so to leave me some time... In fact, don't plan anything for the night's show.

Melinda Gary sits in her office. Susan approaches with a package. She wears blue jeans and a Giants' baseball cap. She looks like the stereotypical delivery kid that rides a bike around San Francisco. She chews bubble gum.

Susan blows a bubble and after it pops, Melinda stands and walks toward Susan. Melinda takes the package and begins opening it immediately.

The package contains two drawings. One is a drawing of Martin standing over a body with Melinda in the background as if she is witnessing the murder. The second one shows a full face of Martin and a full face of Melinda side by side.

The caption reads, "Melinda Gary host of BayTips is Murderer's Accomplice. Anyone knowing the whereabouts of either of these people should call B A Y - T I P S."

Panic stricken from being found out, Melinda runs. As she hurries through the parking garage, Harris jumps out from behind a pillar and grabs her by the arm. He shoves a gun in her ribs, escorts her to his car, and Susan drives away.

Susan, Harris and Melinda get out of his car and Harris ushers Melinda into the D.J.'s studio. Tranby waits there. Harris shoves Melinda into a chair. They brow beat her into telling them that Martin is her brother.

Melinda explains how the Yakuza infiltrated his construction company, sold off the assets, and took the profit from him.

Tranby picks up the phone and dials. She tells Mitchell Fields that she is at D.J.'s Place in Sausalito and that she has Martin Mayhew's accomplice with her.

The blue Chevy drives past the front of D.J.'s Place and slowly pulls into a parking space. Martin and Aaron get out of the car.

Martin tells Aaron to go around back and then continues alone toward the front of the studio. He enters. Martin puts the "CLOSED" sign on the front door and locks it.

At the rear entrance, Aaron approaches the workshop door. He looks around for witnesses, sees none and pulls his gun. He enters the building with gun raised.

Tranby, Susan, Harris and Melinda see Aaron with his gun out and scatter to various parts of the workshop.

Aaron dives behind one of the workbenches and tips it over as a shield.

Tranby runs into the framing room.

Harris sticks his head up, over an art table.

Aaron makes a break for the framing room. Harris pulls his gun and fires at Aaron. He misses.

Susan crashes through the door between the workshop and the lobby. Martin grabs her and puts his gun to her head.

Tranby hides behind a large cabinet that houses mat board stock.

Aaron enters the room, eyes like a rabbit's dart around, he checks the environment. He moves slowly through the room.

Harris runs to the entrance of the framing room. He listens at the door for a moment. He pushes the door open. Aaron spins and fires at the movement of the door.

Harris jumps back against the wall just outside the framing room door.

Aaron moves around the room looking for Tranby. He gets closer to the cabinet where she hides.

Tranby looks around her location for something, anything that might be used as a weapon. She spies a mat cutting knife, like the one introduced in the opening sequence.

Aaron turns the corner, where Tranby was. She's not there.

Tranby comes up from behind Aaron and slashes his neck with the mat cutting knife.

Aaron spins toward her, he points the gun at her. He is at point blank range.

Tranby swings the knife at the gun and hits Aaron in the wrist with the blade. The gun discharges, and falls to the floor. We aren't certain if she was hit.

Tranby and Aaron dive toward the gun. They scuffle as they both try to get the gun. The gun fires again.

Harris pushes the door open. No shot is fired, so he enters the framing room.

Martin pushes Susan through the door into the workshop. He holds her in front of his body as a shield. He moves through the workshop with Susan. There's no movement in the studio.

Then the sound of movement, like a mouse. Melinda sticks her head up from behind a pile of boxes. Martin spins and points his gun in Melinda's direction.

Martin and Susan stand in the middle of the framing room. Tranby and Harris come out from behind a cabinet. Aaron lays dead on the floor.

Tranby throws the mat cutting knife at Martin. He ducks out
of reflex, but loses his grip on Susan. She breaks away.
Martin spins and fires. The bullet hits her in the shoulder.
It throws her to the floor. She scrambles behind a workbench.

In the commotion Tranby moves to a closer angle. She shoots
Martin in the chest with Aaron's gun. He turns and runs
quickly through the door. A gun discharges.

Martin staggers backward through the door and falls face up
at Tranby's feet. He's bleeding profusely. Mitchell Fields
walks through the door, cautiously.

Martin's dying confession reveals that he was hired by
Takayama to assassinate Yamashira.

Fields orders Ross to book Melinda for accessory to murder.
He directs McNally to arrest Takayama. He sends for EMS to
check out Tranby and reminds her and Harris to come to make
statements. Then he heads out to tell Mrs. Yamashira the
news.

Six months later, Harris Richardson stands at Tranby's front
door holding the handset to his ear. Tranby's voice comes
through the speaker.

Harris fidgets nervously, waits for Tranby to decide whether
to let him in or not. Finally, the electronic lock buzzes.
Harris opens the door and enters the building.

Harris struts into her studio carrying a package. He hands
her the package. She tears into the wrapping and out pops a
book. It is entitled "The Tranby Croft Affair" and the cover
shows an artist drawing a crime scene. He asks if she wants
to work on another project? She has a look on her face that
says, "You must be joking."

Scene 14

Marketing Script

Never submit a work in progress. Realize that your script is a prospectus asking for a $10-$30 million investment or more. That is why it must be good.

— David Trottier *The Screenwriter's Bible*

Marketing Script

This draft of the script needs to be your best version. I suggest you proofread it with a partner. Preferably, the partner reads aloud while you follow along. The reader should read all capital letters and punctuation. It might sound like this:

"Fade In, all caps, colon. Master scene heading, exterior period, San Francisco, dash, day all caps. Paragraph, Fog partially covers The Golden Gate Bridge, period. The fog moves fast toward the San Francisco skyline period. Secondary scene heading...."

Once you are certain there are no typos, save it as a .pdf and be prepared to send it to potential buyers.

Here is the final marketing draft of A DEADLY SKETCH.

Enjoy!

"A DEADLY SKETCH"

Written by

Donald E. Simonds

1528 Marketing Script Dr.
Plano, TX 75075
(555) 282-6517
Scriptwriter@sbcglobal.net

"A DEADLY SKETCH"

FADE IN:

EXT. SAN FRANCISCO - DAY

Fog partially covers The Golden Gate Bridge. The fog moves
fast toward the San Francisco skyline.

FISHERMAN'S WHARF

The early afternoon activity around Fisherman's Wharf seems
relatively quiet. Some boats cruise in the bay, a ferry of
visitors heads toward Alcatraz prison.

COIT TOWER

Near Coit Tower some beautiful homes appear to teeter,
precariously perched on the hillsides.

CALIFORNIA STREET

A cable car carries people up the hill toward the Mark
Hopkins Hotel. Passersby stop to look at the unusual
transports.

POLK STREET

Gay men walk hand in hand, arm in arm. Some in drag, others
wear leather and chains.

EXT. THE GOLDEN GATE BRIDGE - NIGHT

As darkness falls, crowds stroll onto the bridge.

FIRE DEPARTMENT BOATS

The fog lifts enough for literally thousands of spectators to
see three fireboats as they start spraying rainbow colored
streams of water from all seven nozzles. The crowd cheers
the traditional fourth of July celebration as San Francisco's
finest turns the show into a colorful water ballet.

A fireworks display spells out "4th of July" then disappears
into smoke. The crowd cheers again.

JAPAN CENTER

The Pagoda looms large above bare streets. The lights of
Japan Center shine bright and the streets fill with more
people moving about. Three tourists enter a restaurant.

EXT. BUCHANAN STREET - NIGHT

MARTIN MAYHEW (45) moves slowly in the shadows near Japan
Center. His mouth opens slightly, his breath visible in the
cool night air. He moves on an apparently aimless course. He
looks average; average build, average height, average
everything.

EXT. OTAFUKU TEI RESTAURANT - REAR DOOR - NIGHT

The back door to the Japanese restaurant swings open and a
tiny man MARIKU YAMASHIRA (60) steps out. A tiny woman, MRS.
YAMASHIRA (55) follows. They wear dinner attire; he in a
suit, she in a cocktail dress.

He weaves like a drunk and she says so. They chatter in
Japanese. The woman throws her hands up and storms back into
the restaurant.

MARTIN

steps out of the shadows. He pulls a .45 caliber hand gun
from his waist band, aims at Mariku Yamashira, and pulls the
trigger.

MARIKU YAMASHIRA

He looks surprised when the shell hits him. He reaches for
his chest and sees blood on his shirt. Martin fires another
shot which hits Yamashira in the head. It explodes blood all
over the wall and forces him into a garbage pile. He dies,
eyes open, lifeless.

INT. POLICE STATION - FIELDS' OFFICE - DAY

DETECTIVE MITCHELL FIELDS (50) sits at his desk, drinks
coffee and stares at the mounds of paperwork which he faces
for the day. He looks like a cowboy, an old Texas Ranger
with gray hair. His face, weathered from years of police
work, appears older than his 50 years.

INSERT - RADIO

                    OSKIE (V.O.)
          Send homicide, forensic, and an
          ambulance to the Buchanan Mall --
          We've got a body at the back door
          of Otafuku Tei, the restaurant
          directly across from the Japan
          Center Pagoda.

BACK TO FIELDS

As he pushes the reports aside, reaches for the phone, and
dials the garage.

                    FIELDS
          This is Fields. Bring my car around
          please.

He pulls on his overcoat, switches off the lights, and leaves
his office.

EXT. CRIME SCENE - NIGHT

The familiar chaos of a crime scene investigation takes shape
as Fields steps from his car. He clips his badge to his coat
and walks to the back door where two ambulance attendants
crouch beside Mariku Yamashira.

The six-man forensic team moves in. Over their shoulders,
Fields sees the victim. Very small, perhaps in his late
fifties, sprawled on his back, arms outstretched. The right
side of his body is covered with blood and half of the man's
face is missing from the impact of the second shot.

                    FIELDS
          Jesus!

Two homicide detectives hover at the outer edge of the
forensic team, ROSS and MCNALLY. Ross (32) tall, gangly
blonde hair, listens to one of the ambulance attendants.

McNally (45) overweight by at least thirty pounds, hair
recedes, gracefully sidesteps a police photographer and
sketches the crime scene on a clipboard pad.

One of the forensic men measures, with a long tape, the
distance from the body to the street; the body to the wall;
the body to the back door of the restaurant. Two other
members of the team poke around in the garbage for evidence.

Across the alley forensic investigators look for anything
the gunman may have dropped.

AMBULANCE

Coroner's attendants hustle the body into a hearse headed for
an autopsy.

CRIME SCENE

investigators rope-off the area, pick up, bag, and tag all
the trace evidence.

One of the men kneels down and with a pair of tweezers, picks
up a brown leather wallet. It evidently had been hidden by
the victim's body until now.

INSERT WALLET

A second pair of tweezers opens it. It contains a wad of
bills.

FIELDS

frowns then nods.

THE WALLET

goes into an evidence bag.

FIELDS

motions to Ross, who watches the scene in silence.

> FIELDS
> What do you make of that?

> ROSS
> What'd ya mean?

> FIELDS
> What do you make of his wallet
> being on the ground, there?

> ROSS
> Nothin' in particular.

> FIELDS
> Did you actually go to some kind of
> detective school?

> ROSS
> Yes actually!

> FIELDS
> Then perhaps you could use your
> deductive training to come up with
> a theory about the wallet!

> ROSS
> (sourly)
> Okay boss.

> FIELDS
> I want to know by ten A.M.

Ross and Fields cross the alley. McNally stands in front of a doorway.

> FIELDS
> Whatcha got?

> MCNALLY
> Shots came from here.

Fields shakes his head.

> FIELDS
> Thirty yards. Must be a hell of a
> marksman. Get any shell casings?

> MCNALLY
> No, must've used a revolver.

> FIELDS
> Hell of a marksman. Who found the
> body?

> MCNALLY
> His wife.

McNally checks his notes.

> MCNALLY
> They'd been arguing. She left him
> out here because he was drunk. A
> few minutes later, she said she
> felt guilty about leaving him out
> here so she came out to apologize
> and found him dead.

> FIELDS
> What time was that?

> MCNALLY
> About nine-forty.

> FIELDS
> Did you interview her?

> MCNALLY
> Of course.

> FIELDS
> She know anyone who might want to
> kill her husband? What was his
> name?

McNally refers to his note pad.

>   MCNALLY
>   Mariku Yamashira. And no. She
>   said he had no enemies.

>   FIELDS
>   Financial difficulties?

>   MCNALLY
>   No. Big no. He was very wealthy.
>   Owned several businesses.

>   ROSS
>   There's your motive, Dude.

>   FIELDS
>   What's the motive?

>   ROSS
>   Big business. We're looking for
>   like a business partner or someone
>   who was like spurned in his
>   business.

>   FIELDS
>   Thanks for that Sherlock.
>   (back to McNally)
>   Any psychiatric problems, domestic
>   trouble, honeys on the side?

>   MCNALLY
>   Not that she was aware of.

>   FIELDS
>   Did you release her?

>   MCNALLY
>   Not yet.

>   FIELDS
>   Okay, take me to her.

INT. OTAFUKU TEI RESTAURANT - NIGHT

The detectives approach Mrs. Yamashira, small of stature with
a proud, calm demeanor.

>   FIELDS
>   Mrs. Yamashira, I'm Mitchell
>   Fields. I'm very sorry about what
>   happened here tonight and I want
>   you to know that I will do
>   everything in my power to bring
>   whoever did this to justice.

Fields hands her his business card with both hands. Mrs.
Yamashira takes the card and reads it.

                    MRS. YAMASHIRA
               (broken English)
          Thank you Detective.

                    FIELDS
          May I ask you something?

                    MRS. YAMASHIRA
          Certainly.

                    FIELDS
          Why did your husband go out to the
          alley?

                    MRS. YAMASHIRA
          We were having an argument. It
          would not be polite to do so in
          public.

                    FIELDS
          I see. That should be all for
          tonight. Would you like one of my
          men to take you home?

                    MRS. YAMASHIRA
          That won't be necessary. I have a
          car waiting, thank you.

                    FIELDS
          Good evening, then.

Fields bows in her direction then leads his team out through
the restaurant the way they came.

INT. COURTROOM - DAY

Crime Illustrator TRANBY CROFT (28) sits shoulders back,
chest out, chin high in the front row of the gallery. She
dresses like a fashion model, very attractive, feminine,
shapely with an athletic body. Her dark brown hair
accentuates her perpetually smiling face. Her eyes,
translucent teal, the most unique shade imaginable,
mesmerize.

She sketches scenarios for the evening news. It's about 10:00
A.M. The prosecutor makes his opening remarks.

Using Design Markers, she draws a scene with the Judge in the
middle and the Prosecutor to the left and the Jury on the
right.

The DEFENSE ATTORNEY and the DEFENDANT sit farthest from the
Jury and, although the PROSECUTOR faces the Jury box, he
points at the accused.

The Prosecuting Attorney takes his seat and the Defense
Attorney approaches the center of the courtroom.

> DEFENSE ATTORNEY
> Ladies and Gentlemen of the Jury.
> My client has been accused of
> murder... premeditated murder... a
> mass murder. It's your job to
> ensure that the Prosecution has
> enough evidence to convict him of
> these crimes... <u>Beyond a shadow of
> doubt.</u> A shadow, that's all. If you
> believe that there is any doubt,
> you must acquit him... Now,

TRANBY

The Defense Attorney's voice drops to barely audible. Tranby
draws a likeness of the Defendant. She takes her eyes off
the sketch pad to look at him for very brief moments. Then
her eyes move quickly back to the pad.

She surveys her work with a pleased expression.

DEFENDANT

His face looks normal, not ugly, but his eyes radiate evil.

INSERT - DRAWING

Tranby works on his eyes, which will be the focal point of
this sketch.

DEFENDANT

turns slightly toward her and smiles a Charles Manson smile.

TRANBY

quickly packs up her materials. Startled by the Defendant's
stare, she scurries down the aisle toward the rear of the
courtroom.

COURTHOUSE HALLWAY

Tranby leaves the courtroom, she leans against the wall, rubs
the back of her neck, as sweat appears on her cheeks.

INT. TV STUDIO - DAY

CHRIS WILLIAMS (35) chubby blonde, talks to Tranby near the
crew. Two crew members move around and fiddle with TV
equipment in the background.

                         CHRIS
              Why are you so upset?

                         TRANBY
              I've never felt so sure someone was
              guilty. The way he looked at me
              sent shivers up my spine.

                         CHRIS
              Why don't we go into my office and
              calm down for awhile.

Tranby squares her shoulders and holds her head high with
confidence.

                         TRANBY
              Thanks, Boss, I'll be Okay. I've
              got lots to do.

TV STATION'S ART STUDIO

Tranby lays out the five sketches from the morning drawings.
She labels them by case and adds a few final touches.

In another part of the room, Tranby struggles with a
particularly large piece of heavy mat board, throwing it onto
the cutting table.

She reaches in the drawer of a supply table and withdraws a
large hook-shaped knife. Tranby cuts five boards large
enough for her sketches, then pastes the sketches to the
board.

INT. SOUND STAGE

In another part of the studio, BRIAN (24) wears pressed blue
jeans and a starched plaid shirt, very preppy. He prepares
the camera equipment and sound stage. He sets up an easel
for Tranby's drawings.

Tranby enters the sound stage carrying her five boards. She
places the first of the boards on the easel.

                         TRANBY
              Okay, Brian, let's shoot this one
              first. It's the opening argument in
              the Gay Rights case.

Brian shoots the picture, then writes the tape number and
time code reading on his log sheet.

> BRIAN
> What will Melinda call this case?

> TRANBY
> The Spect Case.

Brian writes the name of the case on the log.

> BRIAN
> Okay, next sketch.

Tranby removes the first sketch and accidently places the
fourth sketch on the easel. It is the drawing of the evil-
eyed defendant. When she sees what she has done, she winces
in pain.

> TRANBY
> Oh, God!

> BRIAN
> What's wrong?

> TRANBY
> This guy makes me squirm.

> BRIAN
> His eyes are really evil looking.

> TRANBY
> I know. This isn't the next
> picture. I've got two more for the
> Spect case.

They continue shooting drawings.

INT. POLICE STATION - DAY

The hurried pace of any metropolitan police station. Men
quickly walk through with suspects, victims, etc.

MRS. LEE (63) a frail looking Chinese woman, modest
appearance in dress and demeanor, enters the station
cautiously. She looks around for an available officer.

INT. FIELDS' OFFICE

Fields, Ross, and McNally discuss the case.

> FIELDS
> So, Ross, what about the wallet?

                    ROSS
          Nothing.

                    FIELDS
          Nothing? Don't give me that shit.
          There had to be something missing.

                    ROSS
          No, nothing!

                    FIELDS
          Okay, so what else do we have?

                    MCNALLY
          Nothing.

The anger wells up in Fields' face. His face flushes
crimson.

                    FIELDS
          This isn't really making me a happy
          man, McNally.

                    MCNALLY
          I think we have either a pro or a
          serial killer.
               (waits for reaction)
          There was no evidence left at the
          scene of the crime.

                    FIELDS
               (interrupts)
          Well we got the Goddamn head of the
          Yamashira family, don't we? We got
          a bullet. Check that we got two
          bullets. What the fuck caliber is
          the murder weapon?

McNally fires back.

                    MCNALLY
          I meant there was nothing linking
          the murder to a specific suspect.

Fields' face turns a deeper shade of red from McNally's
insubordination. Ross to McNally's rescue.

                    ROSS
          He used a .45, we're checking it
          out.

McNally looks bored.

                    MCNALLY
          Waste of time.

                    FIELDS
          Oh, really?

                    MCNALLY
          He's either a pro or a nut job.
          Either way, we're screwed on
          finding it.

Ross nods agreement.

                    ROSS
          He's right.

                    FIELDS
          Makes sense, but we still gotta
          follow protocol.

                    MCNALLY
          I know.

Ross lost in thought.

                    ROSS
          Why would a wealthy Japanese
          businessman be coming out of the
          rear door of a restaurant?

The phone rings. Fields picks up the receiver.

INTERCUT PHONE CONVERSATION - FIELDS' OFFICE/BYERS' MORGUE

                    FIELDS
          Fields.

                    BYERS
          You better get down here.

                    FIELDS
          What is it?

                    BYERS
          Get down here. You have to see this
          in person.

INT. MORGUE - AUTOPSY ROOM - DAY

Fields, Ross, and McNally enter the autopsy room. BYERS (48)
bald, beer gut, meets them at the door. Without a word, Byers
leads the detectives to the table occupied by Mariku
Yamashira.

Yamashira lays naked, but from a distance appears to be fully clothed. The closer they get the easier it is to determine that Yamashira sports a full body tattoo.

The neckline starts just under his collarbone, extends down his arms to the elbow, covers his complete torso, and ends at his knees.

Although his genitals remain flesh tone, they blend into the scene, almost unnoticeable.

> FIELDS
> What the hell?

> ROSS
> (with delight)
> Yakuza!

> FIELDS
> Ya-what-the?

> ROSS
> Ya-Ku-Za.

Ross moves in to examine the tattoo. An insignia tattooed over the dead man's heart appears to be a medallion.

> FIELDS
> What's that?

> ROSS
> The gang's badge of membership.
> This is too cool, Dude.

> FIELDS
> Don't call me Dude.

> ROSS
> I wasn't calling you Dude. I was
> just saying, like, whoa! Dude. Ya'
> know?

Fields glances around as if looking for what Ross meant, he scratches his head, and drops it.

> FIELDS
> Okay, so what do you mean by the
> gang's badge?

> ROSS
> There are, like, over 100,000
> gangsters in Japan... more than
> 2500 families. Each family has its
> own insignia... like a logo...
> (MORE)

                    ROSS (CONT'D)
          Each member wears a matching lapel
          pin.

                    FIELDS
          How do you know this?

                    ROSS
          Remember about a year ago, The
          President formed his commission on
          organized crime?

                    FIELDS
          Yes go on.

                    ROSS
          Well the reason he did that was
          because organized crime changed...
          no longer exclusively the Mafia.

Ross becomes more animated, uses large gestures as his
excitement builds.

                    ROSS
          In fact, the Mafia only has about
          20,000 gangsters in the United
          States. Shortly after that I read
          an article in Chic magazine that
          talked about...

                    FIELDS
          CHIC Magazine?

                    ROSS
          Yeah, it's good. They have all
          sorts of politically focused
          articles.

                    FIELDS
          You read the articles?

Ross folds his arms in exasperation.

                    ROSS
          Yes, may I continue?

                    FIELDS
          Please.

                    ROSS
          So, there was this article about
          how the Japs were getting revenge
          because of what we did to them in
          World War II.

Ross paces as he struggles to remember the details.

                    ROSS
          It was, like, first came the
          Japanese TVs and stereos and then
          the Japanese cars. They were going
          to, like, cripple our economy.

Ross' excitement builds again to a crescendo.

                    ROSS
          And the most recent and the
          greatest threat was the Yakuza.
          The article said that they were
          taking over the San Francisco, L.
          A., and Las Vegas crime scenes,
          Dude.

                    FIELDS
          You didn't just call me Dude did
          you?

                    ROSS
          No.

Ross points at the tattooed man.

                    ROSS
          So, he's Yakuza.

                    MCNALLY
          We need to consult with John
          McGwire.

                    FIELDS
          Why?

                    MCNALLY
          He heads the Special Gang Task
          Force. He might be able to give us
          some insight into the Yakuza in the
          Bay Area.

                    FIELDS
          Good thinking. Set it up.

McNally nods. The detectives shake Byers' hand.

                    FIELDS
          Jim, would you get me a nice 8 x 10
          glossy of that emblem and the body
          tattoo as well, so I can show it to
          McGwire.

                    BYERS
          Be on your desk in an hour.

                    ROSS
          One Hour Photo, cool!

Fields gives Ross a dirty look, as the three detectives leave
the autopsy room.

INT. FIELDS' OFFICE

BEN BROWN (30) wears a patrolman's uniform, enters the
doorway with Mrs. Lee.

                    BEN
          Detective Fields?

Ben looks around Fields' empty office.

                    FIELDS
              Yes?

Ben turns, not knowing where the voice came from startles him
momentarily. He sees Fields, Ross, and McNally approach in
the hallway.

                    BEN
          Oh, there you are. This is Mrs.
          Lee. Says she saw your shooter.

All three detectives pick up the pace.

                    FIELDS
          Come right in Mrs. Lee.
              (to Ross)
          Help Mrs. Lee to your chair.
              (to Ben)
          Thank you Patrolman.

Fields takes a sheet of paper from Ben.

                    MRS. LEE
              (to Ross)
          Thank you.

Fields begins to interrogate the witness. Mrs. Lee speaks
with a heavy accent, pronounces all "ls" like "rs".

                    FIELDS
          It says here you live in Sausalito
          and why were you in the city last
          night?

                    MRS. LEE
          My husband and I were coming in for
          dinner.

                    FIELDS
          So where were you when it happened?

                    MRS. LEE
          At the end of the arrey.

                    FIELDS
          Your husband saw this too?

                    MRS. LEE
          Yes.

                    FIELDS
          Why isn't he here with you?

                    MRS. LEE
          He didn't want to get invorrved.

                    FIELDS
          I see. He didn't want to get
          involved, but he wanted you to get
          involved?

                    MRS. LEE
          No. He doesn't know I'm here. He
          tord me to stay out of it.

                    ROSS
          Well, we sure are glad you came
          down, Mrs. Lee. If you were at the
          mouth of the alley, what did you
          see exactly?

The detectives look at each other with heightened
anticipation.

                    MRS. LEE
          First, I heard a roud bang noise.
          Then I rooked down the arrey and
          saw a man standing at the back door
          of Otafuku Tei near the garbage
          cans.

She appears very calm and confident.

                    MCNALLY
          Then what happened?

                    MRS. LEE
          Then I heard another bang noise,
          and another man stepped out of the
          shadows from the opposite side of
          the arrey.

                    ROSS
          You were pretty far away, can you
          identify this man.

                    MRS. LEE
          Oh yes! I never forget those eyes.

                    FIELDS
          Is there anything else you can tell
          us about the shooting?

                    MRS. LEE
          No. It all happened very fast.

                    FIELDS
          I'm sure it did, but you're certain
          that you can identify the man.

                    MRS. LEE
          Yes! Absorootry!

                    MCNALLY
          Did you see the gun?

                    MRS. LEE
          No, onry the face.

                    FIELDS
          We'll show you some mug shots to
          see if you can pick him out. I'd
          also like to ask you to describe
          the man to an artist. Would you do
          that?

                    MRS. LEE
          Will it take rong? I do need to
          meet my husband for runch. I don't
          want him to get suspicious.

                    FIELDS
          It shouldn't take too long.
               (to Ross)
          Get Tranby Croft down here.
               (to Mrs. Lee)
          Tranby works with the "BayTips"
          program to help us find fugitives
          and such.
                    (MORE)

                    FIELDS (CONT'D)
              (to McNally)
          Take Mrs. Lee to look at mug shots.

MOMENTS LATER

Tranby Croft enters Fields' office like no other. She beams
with enthusiasm for life.

                    TRANBY
          Hi Mitch.

                    FIELDS
          Tranby, my name is Mitchell, not
          Mitch. You may call me Detective
          Fields or Mitchell, but stop
          calling me Mitch.

                    TRANBY
          Right, so what do we have here,
          Mitch --

She sees the disgust on the Detective's face.

                    TRANBY
          -- ell. Anyway, what do you want me
          for?

Fields escorts Tranby to the mug shot room.

INT. MUG SHOT ROOM - DAY

Mrs. Lee and McNally sit at a table strewn with mug shot
books. Fields and Tranby enter and he introduces Tranby to
Mrs. Lee.

                    FIELDS
          Tranby, this is Mrs. Lee. She saw a
          killer who is on the loose and
          thinks she can ID him. I told her
          about BayTips and wanted you to
          draw this guy.

Tranby extends her hand to Mrs. Lee. They shake.

                    TRANBY
          Hi, I'm Tranby Croft.

Mrs. Lee bows slightly in respect of Tranby's esteem.

                    TRANBY
          Generally BayTips sketches are of
          the crime scene to get people to
          come forward, Mrs. Lee.

                    FIELDS
          Well in this case, we have an eye
          witness. Now we want someone to
          come forward if they see this guy.
          We'd like it on this evening's
          show.

                    TRANBY
          Okay, Mitch -- ell, I'll try.

INT. POLICE STATION - ANOTHER OFFICE - DAY

Tranby and Mrs. Lee sit alone in a vacant office. Tranby
tries to make Mrs. Lee feel safe. She uses a non-threatening
interview method. Tranby starts to make sketches.

SERIES OF SHOTS - TRANBY CONSTRUCTS A PORTRAIT

A)   Tranby asks Mrs. Lee about basic head shape.

B)   The face starts to appear.

C)   They sit side-by-side Tranby adds hair to the sketch.

D)   Tranby tacks the drawing to the wall and they examine it.

E)   Finally, Mrs. Lee approves the sketch.

INT. FIELDS' OFFICE

Tranby sticks her head into Mitchell's office.

                    TRANBY
          Got it! I'm on my way to the
          station.

                    FIELDS
          We need one to circulate.

                    TRANBY
          Okay, but I've got to hurry.

Mitchell jumps up and runs for the door, snags the drawing
from Tranby's hand, and the two race down the hall toward the
copy room.

INT. COPY ROOM - DAY

The first copy comes out of the machine. Mitchell picks it
out of the tray.

                    FIELDS
          This one is clean, thanks.

EXT. YAMASHIRA MANSION - NIGHT

The Yamashira mansion perches like a monument to wealth on
the Tiburon Coast.

INT. YAMASHIRA MANSION - NIGHT

From the great room window, the most spectacular view
imaginable, a panorama of San Francisco Bay from Emeryville
to the Golden Gate Bridge and everything in between.

At 7 p.m. the procession of Oyabun, the top Yakuza bosses,
streams into the great room. All thin and short, wear the
same shiny suits with a lapel pin that matches the tattoo on
Yamashira's chest.

Each of the twelve members of the Board of Directors places a
tribute in an ornate bowl, positioned at the entrance to the
great room.

All the men sit in the lavish living-room furniture. Mrs.
Yamashira stands at the hearth.

                    MRS. YAMASHIRA
               (in Japanese)
          Please Gentlemen, make yourselves
          comfortable. As you know, my
          husband was murdered last night.
          Our purpose tonight is to decide
          what to do about that and to begin
          the selection process for a
          successor.

OSUKA (58) distinguished, commands respect, stands to address
Mrs. Yamashira.

                    OSUKA
          Yamashira-sama, with all due
          respect, I believe we need to
          appoint a successor before we can
          decide what to do about your
          husband's death.

TAKAYAMA (55), also distinguished, but larger, more menacing
than Osuka, stands.

                    TAKAYAMA
          If we are to vote, I suggest that
          we take nominations from the board
          of directors.

                    MRS. YAMASHIRA
          Gentlemen, please. My husband left
          strict instructions on how we would
          conduct this meeting and I intend
          to honor his request.

The two generals return to their seats.

Each board member opens an envelope and withdraws a single
sheet of paper.

                    MRS. YAMASHIRA
          First, my husband has outlined his
          request for the funeral and burial,
          which should take place between the
          fourth and sixth day after his
          death. Since the police have not
          contacted me yet, we cannot make
          funeral arrangements. Hopefully,
          they will release him soon, so we
          can have the funeral on Monday or
          Tuesday. I will notify everyone as
          soon as my husband's body is
          released.

Now she reads from the instruction sheet.

                    MRS. YAMASHIRA
          Here are the rules: One; no
          lobbying for votes. Two; no
          election until after burial, and I
          might reiterate, no election until
          we have concluded our business with
          his murderer. Three; each board
          member will name the individual who
          best represents the values of giri-
          ninjo of obligation and compassion,
          and several characteristics of an
          exceptional leader. Four; a two-
          thirds majority vote is required,
          and I will lead the voting process,
          when the time comes.

Everyone nods agreement.

                    MRS. YAMASHIRA
          Now let's look at the
          characteristics you should
          consider. They are listed on the
          back of this paper.

Everyone turns the page over as she continues.

                    MRS. YAMASHIRA
          These are listed in order of
          importance to the job. They are:
          obligation and compassion,
          judgment, operational planning,
          leadership and influence, and
          compatibility of personal values
          with the values of the
          organization. Do you have any
          questions?

Silence, Mrs. Yamashira adjourns the meeting. Each board
member approaches her to convey his sympathy for her loss,
then departs.

INT. HARRIS RICHARDSON'S APARTMENT - NIGHT

HARRIS RICHARDSON (32) suave and debonair, tall and fit,
could have been a basketball player, sits in front of his
television watching the eleven o'clock news.

INSERT - T.V. SCREEN

MELINDA GARY (38), stereotypical news anchor, gives her
report.

                    MELINDA
          Crime Illustrator, Tranby Croft,
          has developed this sketch based
          upon an eye witness account.

The drawing fills the screen.

                    MELINDA (V.O.)
          Should you see this man, please
          call BayTips...

The letters "BayTips" are SUPERIMPOSED on the T.V. screen.
Under each letter is the corresponding number, "229-8477."

BACK TO HARRIS

Harris watches the report.

                    HARRIS
          Susan, come here.

                    MELINDA (V.O.)
          ...that's 229-8477.

The drawing moves behind Melinda, so both the reporter and
the murderer can be seen on the T.V. screen.

SUSAN (30) tall like Harris, might have been a runner-up in
the Miss California contest several years earlier, would have
undoubtedly won the swimsuit competition. She sticks her head
into the room.

> HARRIS
> Sis, watch this. It's what I've
> been looking for.

> SUSAN
> A case?

> MELINDA (V.O.)
> Remember this man is considered
> armed and dangerous. If you see
> him, do not try to interfere, just
> call B.A.Y.T.I.P.S, 229-8477.

> HARRIS
> I'm going to have to meet this
> Tranby Croft.

> SUSAN
> Who's Tranby Croft?

> HARRIS
> The Illustrator.

> SUSAN
> Interesting angle. I can see why
> you're excited.

Susan goes to the telephone stand and picks up a directory.
She flips through the pages.

> SUSAN
> There is a T. Croft on Sacramento
> Street.

INT. TRANBY'S APARTMENT - STUDIO - DAY

Tranby bends over the art table within her apartment
developing some drawings for the BayTips show. The intercom
buzzes. She straightens up and starts for the door. Stops.
Adds just a little more color to the sketch. Hesitates. Then
proceeds to the door constantly looks back at the drawing
until she leaves the room.

HALLWAY - FRONT DOOR

She lifts the telephone handset.

EXT. TRANBY'S BUILDING

Harris Richardson stands at the front door holding a handset
to his ear. Tranby's voice comes through the speaker.

                    TRANBY (O.S.)
          Who is it?

                    HARRIS
          Harris Richardson. I'm looking for
          Tranby Croft.

                    TRANBY (O.S.)
          You found her. What do you want?

                    HARRIS
          I'm a writer and I'd like to talk
          to you.

                    TRANBY (O.S.)
          Chronicle?

                    HARRIS
          Novels.

                    TRANBY (O.S.)
          I'm busy!

                    HARRIS
          Wait!

                    TRANBY (O.S.)
          What is it you want?

                    HARRIS
          I just need a couple of minutes.
          I'd like to learn about your role
          in crime investigations.

                    TRANBY (O.S.)
          Why me?

                    HARRIS
          I think it would be an interesting
          angle for my next novel.

Silence. Harris fidgets nervously.

                    HARRIS
          You still there?

                    TRANBY (O.S.)
          I'm thinking. I'm on my way
          downtown, but I'll give you five
          minutes at the coffee shop at the
          corner of Polk. Okay?

                    HARRIS
          Good enough.

Harris hangs up the phone, trots down the stoop and heads
toward Polk Street.

INT. TRANBY'S APARTMENT - STUDIO

She runs through her studio to the front window and peers out
to see Harris. He turns his head, glances up the street for
approaching cars, as he crosses Sacramento Street and she
gets a good look at his face, a kind face.

INT. PEETS COFFEE SHOP - DAY

Tranby approaches Harris.

                    TRANBY
          Mr. Richardson?

Harris looks up, makes eye contact, pauses and tries not to
smile like men do when lust destroys their brains. His eyes
sparkle as he gazes upon Tranby Croft for the first time.
The object of his most passionate desires stands before him.

                    HARRIS
          Harris Richardson.

He extends his hand in a business-like greeting.

                    HARRIS
          Pleased to meet you.

                    TRANBY
          Listen, I only have a minute. I've
          got to get these sketches to the TV
          studio.

She opens her portfolio wide enough for Harris to see the
drawings, but not the rest of the Coffee Shop patrons.

                    TRANBY
          Maybe you should tell me a little
          bit about your proposal.

Harris begins to explain.

                    HARRIS
               (proudly)
          I write mystery and suspense
          novels, which are based on real-
          life murders.

Harris moves in his chair.

                    HARRIS
          I'd like to get your help in re-
          creating all the crimes that this
          guy has committed so I can write
          about this particular case.

                    TRANBY
          What guy?

Fidgets in his chair.

                    HARRIS
          The guy they showed on BayTips last
          night. The one you drew from an
          eyewitness.

                    TRANBY
          How did you know I drew it?

                    HARRIS
          The lady on Channel 2 gave you
          credit as the crime illustrator. I
          thought it would be a great angle
          on a new book, and --

Tranby stiffens up.

                    TRANBY
          -- Wait a minute, did you say
          Melinda gave me credit?

                    HARRIS
          Yeah, so?

                    TRANBY
          She's not suppose to do that... Are
          you sure she mentioned my name?

                    HARRIS
          Absolutely, how do you think I
          found you?

                    TRANBY
          Well, I'm going to have a word with
          Ms. Melinda Gary.

INT. T.V. STUDIO - DAY

A crew member clips Melinda's microphone to the inside of her blouse. She looks down at his hands and then up quickly at his eyes. Her look scolds him for fondling her intentionally during the procedure.

Tranby storms onto the set.

>   DIRECTOR
>   Tranby, clear the set. We have five
>   seconds.

>   TRANBY
>   (to Melinda)
>   Don't you use my name again.

>   DIRECTOR
>   Four. Three.

>   MELINDA
>   (disgusted)
>   I won't.

>   DIRECTOR
>   Two. One.

>   MELINDA
>   (almost snarling)
>   For God Sake.

The Director points his finger at Melinda, mouths the words.

>   DIRECTOR
>   You're on.

Melinda's expression changes to a big Hollywood smile.

>   MELINDA
>   Good evening. This is
>   BayTips. I'm Melinda Gary.

TRANBY AND HARRIS

Melinda reports faintly in the background. A crew member changes Tranby's drawings being shot by another T.V. camera to stage left of Melinda. A monitor in front of Harris shows the magic of television. He sees what actually goes out over the airwaves.

>   HARRIS
>   Absolutely fascinating.

                    TRANBY
          Okay. I'll do it.

                    HARRIS
          You'll work with me?

                    TRANBY
          Sure. It sounds like fun.

                    HARRIS
          Great. Let's go to dinner and
          celebrate.

Harris gets closer.

                    TRANBY
          No!

                    HARRIS
          Why not?

                    TRANBY
          Maybe tomorrow. I'm exhausted.

EXT. TRANBY'S BUILDING - NIGHT

Twenty minutes later the couple stands at the front door of
her apartment building. They face each other.

                    TRANBY
          Thank you for escorting me home.

                    HARRIS
          It's still early.

Tranby extends her hand to shake on the deal.

                    TRANBY
          I'll see you tomorrow.

Harris takes her hand, places his business card in her palm.

                    HARRIS
          Here's my number if you need
          anything or your plans change.

With a sparkle in Tranby's eye, she unlocks the outside door
and steps in. Harris waits for the door to close, hears the
lock click, then walks down the stoop and out of sight.

INT. TRANBY'S APARTMENT - HALLWAY

She walks in, drops her purse on the floor, almost in a
trance. As she heads to the bedroom, she kicks off her shoes.

Then her dress comes off. Panty-hose are next and she sighs
as the pressure releases. Then the bra and another sigh.

BATHROOM

Tranby brushes her teeth.

BEDROOM

She hops into bed, slips under the sheets, Tranby lays there
for a few moments. She smiles a warm cuddly kind of smile and
rolls over. She reaches for the light and turns it off. The
room darkens. Some street noise filters into her room, but
otherwise everything is still.

She breathes deeply, her eyes move beneath the lids,
indicating a dream state. The serenity breaks from the loud
ring of the telephone. It startles her. The second rings
louder. She sits up abruptly and answers the phone.

> TRANBY
> (weakly)
> Hello?

> MARTIN
> Ms. Croft?

> TRANBY
> Yes?

> MARTIN
> I'm the man you've been drawing and
> I want you to stop putting my
> picture on the BayTips program. I
> know you like me, and the drawings
> of my adventures are very nice, but
> if I see my face on Channel 2
> again, YOU'RE DEAD. Understand?

The phone clicks dead, followed by a dial tone. Tranby's eyes
fill with tears and her face turns pallid.

INT. FIELDS' OFFICE - DAY

JOHN MCGWIRE (42) looks more like a politician than a cop.
He enters Fields' office with the authoritative posture of a
Governor.

> MCGWIRE
> Inspector John McGwire. You wanted
> to see me?

McGwire extends his hand to Fields. As they shake.

                    FIELDS
          Yes, John, thanks. They tell me
          you're heading up the Gang Task
          Force.

                    MCGWIRE
          That's right.

                    FIELDS
          We're investigating a murder and
          wanted to get your take on it.

Fields hands the pictures of Yamashira's naked, tattooed body
to McGwire.

                    MCGWIRE
          Oh yeah, Yakuza.

                    FIELDS
          His name is --

                    MCGWIRE
          Mariku Yamashira.

                    FIELDS
          You know him?

                    MCGWIRE
          Absolutely, We've been
          investigating him for two years.
          Can't make a case stick. Reluctant
          witnesses.

                    FIELDS
          You mind if I get a couple of my
          detectives to sit in on this
          meeting?

                    MCGWIRE
          Not at all.

                    FIELDS
          Great, have a seat.

Fields points to a chair, as he picks up the telephone and
dials.

                    FIELDS
          Ross, grab McNally and come to my
          office. John McGwire is here.

MOMENTS LATER

the two detectives briskly enter the office and slam into
their chairs.

                    FIELDS
          So, John, we were hoping you could
          fill us in on what you know about
          the Yakuza. Maybe help us
          strategize on ways to get to the
          bottom of this murder.

                    MCGWIRE
          Okay, perhaps I should start with a
          little history. They have been
          around at least as long as the
          American Mafia, probably longer.

McGwire moves to a chalk board and writes "30's" and "40's"
on it.

                    MCGWIRE
          We have some knowledge of incidents
          that took place in the thirties and
          forties.

He writes 1976 on the board.

                    MCGWIRE
          We became acutely aware of them
          around nineteen seventy-six.

On the left column he writes their "Primary Businesses" as he
speaks them.

                    MCGWIRE
          Their primary businesses are
          prostitution, porn, drugs, and
          gambling.

On the right column he writes "Appear Legit."

                    MCGWIRE
          But to appear legit, they also have
          purchased large chunks of
          construction, real estate, and
          entertainment industries.

He writes, "mizu shobai" on the board.

                    MCGWIRE
          They bought "the water businesses"
          bars, restaurants, night clubs.
                    (MORE)

                    MCGWIRE (CONT'D)
          That's how they launder their
          illicit profits.

                    FIELDS
          What are we looking for?

                    MCGWIRE
          They travel in packs. The <u>Oyabun</u>
          or Father figure is usually
          surrounded by <u>Kobun</u> the Child
          figure. They carry his bags, light
          his cigarettes and say '<u>hai, hai</u>' a
          lot.

                    FIELDS
          Hai, Hai?

                    MCGWIRE
          It means "yes" in Japanese. They
          are his little "Yes Men," punks
          really. In fact, the elders call
          them <u>Chimpira</u>.

                    FIELDS
          Chimps?

                    MCGWIRE
          No, it's slang for penis, like we
          might call someone a "little
          prick."

The detectives all laugh, uncomfortably.

                    MCGWIRE
          Of course you could get lucky and
          spot a missing pinkie.

                    FIELDS
          Missing pinkie?

                    MCGWIRE
          <u>Yubitsume</u>. If a Yakuza member
          offends another, particularly a
          <u>Oyabun</u>, the offender is obliged to
          lose the finger or lose face.

John stands to demonstrate. He pulls a pocket knife from his
pants, opens it, places his left hand on Fields' desk, pulls
the knife toward himself, and leans all his body weight down
on the knife. With a bone cracking noise he falls back into
his chair.

The detectives gasp. Then John shows his finger is still
intact.

                    MCGWIRE
          Just kidding. But the finger is
          then sent to the offended party as
          an apology.

                    FIELDS
          Seriously?

                    MCGWIRE
          Seriously!

After a brief moment, Fields changes the subject.

                    FIELDS
          What can you tell us about
          Yamashira?

                    MCGWIRE
          Mariku came to the United States,
          having already established himself
          as head of a syndicate in Osaka.

McGwire takes his seat.

                    MCGWIRE
          His basic MO... find a company in
          financial trouble, engage schemes
          to take it over, and sell off the
          assets... big profit.

                    FIELDS
          But you haven't had any luck
          nailing him?

                    MCGWIRE
          No, he isn't, wasn't hands on at
          his level. We're shooting
          surveillance video at a place
          called Bay Area Restaurant Supply.

                    FIELDS
          Mind if we join the stake out?

McGwire takes a business card and writes down the address of
the surveillance location.

                    MCGWIRE
          I'll tell 'em you'll be there
          tonight.

John stands to leave and hands the card to Fields.

                    MCGWIRE
          If there's nothing else, I need to
          get back?

                    FIELDS
          We appreciate the education. We'll
          be there tonight around ten-thirty.

They all shake hands and McGwire leaves.

EXT. YAMASHIRA MANSION - DAY

Fields rings the doorbell at the Yamashira mansion. A
SERVANT answers the door. Fields hands her his card. The
woman invites him in and escorts him to the great room.

INT. YAMASHIRA MANSION

The servant encourages him to take a seat then leaves. A few
moments later, Mrs. Yamashira enters the room.

                    MRS. YAMASHIRA
          Hello, Detective, welcome to my
          home.

Fields stands.

                    FIELDS
          It's very lovely, Mrs. Yamashira.

                    MRS. YAMASHIRA
          To what do I owe this pleasure?

                    FIELDS
          I have a few questions I would like
          to ask you.

                    MRS. YAMASHIRA
          Very well.

She motions for him to sit and she takes a seat near his.

                    FIELDS
          First, I wanted you to know I have
          a suspect.

                    MRS. YAMASHIRA
          I saw his picture on the news
          program.

Fields takes one of the composites from his note folder and
hands it to her.

                    FIELDS
          Do you recognize him?

She looks at it very intensely.

                    MRS. YAMASHIRA
          No, I am afraid not.

She hands the picture back to him.

                    FIELDS
          We believe he had some business
          connection with your husband.

Mrs. Yamashira stares at Fields, but says nothing. Fields
fidgets in his chair.

                    FIELDS
               (Awkwardly)
          Are you sure you've never seen him
          before?

                    MRS. YAMASHIRA
          I am certain.

                    FIELDS
          What kind of work was your husband
          in?

                    MRS. YAMASHIRA
          In our culture, women are
          subservient, eager to obey. I
          would not presume to ask about my
          husband's business.

                    FIELDS
          You have no idea how he made his
          money?

                    MRS. YAMASHIRA
          He owned several businesses, but I
          wouldn't know the details.

                    FIELDS
          Did he own Otafuku Tei?

                    MRS. YAMASHIRA
          Yes, I believe he did.

                    FIELDS
          Why were you there on the night of
          his murder?

                    MRS. YAMASHIRA
          To have dinner, of course.

                    FIELDS
          You weren't meeting anyone else?

                    MRS. YAMASHIRA
          No, we eat there often. You may
          ask the manager. His name is
          Takayama.

                    FIELDS
          I will. One last thing, for now,
          um, during the autopsy, we couldn't
          help but notice that your husband
          has a full body tattoo. What can
          you tell me about that?

                    MRS. YAMASHIRA
          In Japan there are many customs
          that Americans do not share and do
          not understand. Each of the scenes
          in my husband's body art was placed
          there for a reason; perhaps to ward
          off evil spirits or to bring luck
          to the family. The application of
          this tattoo was extensive and
          painful.   It took hundreds of
          hours and was considered a test of
          his mettle.

Fields reaches into his note folder and withdraws the close-
up of the insignia on Yamashira's chest. He hands the
photograph to her.

                    FIELDS
          What does this represent?

                    MRS. YAMASHIRA
          I'm afraid I don't know the
          significance of that.

                    FIELDS
          Mrs. Yamashira, I think you know
          very well what this is. I think
          your husband was the leader of the
          Yakuza syndicate and the person
          that murdered him had been wronged
          by your husband in some way.

                    MRS. YAMASHIRA
          First of all, the Yakuza are a
          necessary vice for Japanese
          society.
                         (MORE)

                    MRS. YAMASHIRA (CONT'D)
          They were underdog folk heroes who
          stood up for the poor and the
          defenseless, like your Anglo-
          American myth of Robin Hood.

                    FIELDS
          You're telling me that the Yakuza
          is a myth?

                    MRS. YAMASHIRA
          For all practical purposes, yes.
          My husband worked very hard to
          change the perception of Yakuza.
          He was an entrepreneur. He was
          clean. He pay taxes. You will not
          find any criminal record or
          evidence of any criminal activity.

                    FIELDS
          All right Mrs. Yamashira, have it
          your way. I will find this man
          with or without your help and I
          will put him behind bars. But if I
          find out you're withholding
          evidence from me, I'll put you
          behind bars as well. Do you
          understand me?

Fields stands ready to leave.

                    MRS. YAMASHIRA
          When may I have my husband?

                    FIELDS
          They didn't call you?

                    MRS. YAMASHIRA
          No. I can't schedule the funeral
          arrangements until I know when his
          body will be released.

                    FIELDS
          I'm sorry. He should have been
          released yesterday. I'm sure he is
          ready by now. You can get him on
          Monday at the latest and schedule
          the funeral for Tuesday, if you
          like.

                    MRS. YAMASHIRA
          Thank You.

                    FIELDS
          I want to help you. You need to
          help me.

                    MRS. YAMASHIRA
          I understand, detective.

EXT. TRANBY'S BUILDING - NIGHT

Martin waits in the passenger seat of a light blue '68 Chevy
Impala on Sacramento Street.

INT. CAR

Next to him AARON BANKS (30) barely fits behind the steering
wheel. A large man, not at all attractive, greased-back
hair, dark eyes, olive skin, swigs Jack Daniels straight from
the bottle.

                    MARTIN
          That's it over there, the apartment
          on the third floor, street side.

EXT. CAR

A TALL MAN and a SEXY WOMAN cross in front of the Impala
toward Tranby's apartment building.

Martin and Aaron jump out of the car and speed walk toward
the apartment building. They turn into the front stoop of
Tranby's building.

The Tall Man opens the door and the couple enter the
building.

MARTIN AND AARON

jump onto the stoop. Martin goes immediately to the phone as
Aaron puts his foot just in the door jam so it won't close
all the way.

THE COUPLE

The Tall Man turns quickly startled by the noise.

REVERSE ANGLE

Martin looks away about 45 degrees from the door. The man can
not see Martin's face. Aaron turns his back toward the door
and looks directly at Martin.

INSERT - AARON'S SHOE

Heal in the threshold. As the door closes it clicks, but the
door stops 1/4 inch short of latching.

BACK ON AARON

He pulls a comb from his pocket and combs his hair. The Tall
Man inside the building turns away, puts his arm around Sexy
Woman, and continues into the building. Obviously satisfied
that the door did latch.

INT. TRANBY'S BUILDING

As soon as the couple are out of sight Martin and Aaron run
into the building up the first flight of stairs.

THIRD FLOOR HALLWAY

At Tranby's Apartment Door, they knock and wait a moment
before breaking the lock.

INT. TRANBY'S APARTMENT

They move cautiously into the apartment, explore quietly
through. Aaron goes to the right and Martin goes to the left.

MARTIN

heads toward the bedroom. No one in there. He comes out and
into the kitchen. No one there either.

AARON

sticks his head around the wall into the living room. He
makes eye contact with Martin.

                         AARON
              No one here.

Martin walks into the living room.

MARTIN

sits down on the sofa and lights a cigarette.

                    AARON
          Let's get outta here.

                    MARTIN
          It's not that late, I say we wait
          for her.

                    AARON
          What if she doesn't come back all
          night... I got to go to work in the
          morning.

                    MARTIN
          We wait.

EXT. TRANBY'S BUILDING - NIGHT

Tranby and Harris stand outside the building looking at the
front door, which is slightly ajar.

Harris pushes the door with his finger. It opens softly. They
look at each other suspiciously, but enter the building.

THIRD FLOOR HALLWAY

Tranby and Harris examine the door.

INSERT - LOCK

Scratched and obviously burgled.

BACK TO SCENE

Tranby and Harris look at each other.

                    HARRIS
          Call the police.

Tranby and Harris scamper down the stairs.

EXT. TRANBY'S BUILDING - NIGHT

Tranby and Harris race off the stoop and into Sacramento
Street.

INSERT - CELL PHONE

Harris dials 911.

MOMENTS LATER

a patrol car pulls up in front of Tranby's building.

INT. TRANBY'S APARTMENT

Aaron stands at the front window.

                AARON
       Cops are here.

Martin crushes his cigarette into an ashtray.

                MARTIN
       Shit. Let's get outta here.

Aaron sprints to the front door.

                MARTIN
       Not that way.

Martin leads Aaron to a back door in the apartment.

EXT. TRANBY'S APARTMENT - BACK PORCH

The two partners descend a wooden stair case from the third
floor, which goes all the way down to ground level just as

INT. TRANBY'S APARTMENT - FRONT DOOR

Two officers pull their weapons. TWEETY (29) male and OSKIE
(30) female enter the apartment. Quickly search throughout,
find nothing.

When they get back to the front door where Tranby and Harris
wait.

                TWEETY
       Okay, it's secure. You can come in
       now.

Tranby and Harris enter the apartment.

Tweety places his weapon in it's holster.

                    TWEETY
          Don't touch anything. I'm going to
          call Detective Fields and the
          forensic team.

                    TRANBY
          What's the matter?

                    OSKIE
          Do you smoke?

                    TRANBY
          No, why do you ask?

                    OSKIE
          I saw a cigarette butt in the
          ashtray in the living room. It
          smells fresh.

                    TRANBY
          I don't own an ashtray.

                    OSKIE
          Well, you know what I mean.

                    TRANBY
          No, I don't. Are you saying the
          sonofabitch put a cigarette out in
          some of my china?

LIVING ROOM

A forensic man examines the chair where Martin had been
sitting. He dusts for fingerprints. Another man picks up the
cigarette with a pair of tweezers.

DINING ROOM

Tranby and Harris sit at the dining room table, when Fields,
McNally, and Ross enter the room and pull up chairs.

                    FIELDS
          Well Tranby, we'll be interviewing
          the rest of the tenants now. I'll
          check back with you before I leave.

                    TRANBY
          Thanks Mitchell.

Fields pauses a moment to register that she called him
Mitchell.

                    FIELDS
          Forensic should be finishing up
          soon and I'll station a patrolman
          outside your door for your safety.
          Can I get you anything else now?

                    TRANBY
          No thanks, I appreciate your help.

                    FIELDS
          Hey, it's the least I could do.

                    ROSS
          Tranby, that drawing must be very
          accurate. We've got him scared.
          It's just a matter of time now.

THIRD FLOOR HALLWAY

The three detectives leave Tranby's apartment. They close the
door behind them. In the hall they confer.

                    FIELDS
          Ross, I want you to wait outside.
          When that Harris Richardson fellow
          leaves, tail him. I want to know
          about his every move.

                    ROSS
          You think he's involved?

                    FIELDS
          Do you buy that crap about the
          novelist just wants a story?

                    ROSS
          Seemed sincere.

                    FIELDS
          Tail his butt.

                    ROSS
          Yes Sir.

                    FIELDS
          McNally, lets start knocking on
          doors.

DINING ROOM

Harris stands to leave.

                    HARRIS
          I need to get home.

He pecks her check. She hugs him close.

>   TRANBY
>   Don't go.

He has to break her grip.

>   HARRIS
>   I'll call you later, when all the
>   cops are gone.

EXT. TRANBY'S BUILDING - NIGHT

Harris walks down Sacramento Street. Ross follows.

Ross jumps into an unmarked car and follows Harris very
slowly.

Harris maneuvers his large frame into a late model Firebird
and takes off like a bat out of hell.

EXT. SPORTING GOODS STORE

Harris enters the store. Ross pulls in beside the store and
gets out of his car. Ross sneaks up to the window and looks
in.

INT. SPORTING GOODS STORE

Harris puts a .38 calibre hand gun on the counter. The CLERK
rings up the sale, including some shells.

INT. UNMARKED CAR

Ross goes back to his car and picks up the mic to his car
radio.

>   ROSS
>   This is 1 David 5 can you patch me
>   through to Detective Fields.

>   RADIO DISPATCHER (V.O.)
>   Roger.

Ross watches Harris leave the store.

>   RADIO DISPATCHER (V.O.)
>   Go ahead detective.

>   FIELDS (V.O.)
>   Fields here.

                    ROSS
          It's Ross. Our boy is just leaving
          a sporting goods store. He bought a
          gun.

                    FIELDS (V.O.)
          I wonder why he did that?

                    ROSS
          Maybe he doesn't want us to ID the
          same weapon from the other murders.

                    FIELDS (V.O.)
          Possibly. Thanks Ross. Where are
          you now, young man?

The two cars pull away.

                    ROSS
          I'm tailing him.

                    FIELDS (V.O.)
          Let me know when and where he
          lights and I'll send back-up.

                    ROSS
          Roger. Out.

INT. TRANBY'S APARTMENT - LIVING ROOM - NIGHT

Detective Fields and Tranby sit in the living room.

                    FIELDS
          All I'm saying is that you should
          be cautious. If your Mr. Richardson
          isn't involved, then great! But,
          what if he is?

                    TRANBY
          That's impossible. He's been with
          me all day long.

                    FIELDS
          I'm not accusing him of --

                    TRANBY
          -- Sounds like it to me.

There is a long moment of silence.

                    FIELDS
          Okay, let's think for a minute.
          What do you know about him?

                    TRANBY
          Not much, I just met him yesterday.

                    FIELDS
          Did he tell you he had a run in
          with SFPD?

                    TRANBY
          He told me he uncovered
          incriminating evidence against a
          rather prominent detective.

                    FIELDS
          He accused ex-Sergeant Nathan Burns
          of taking bribes.

                    TRANBY
          Was he guilty?

                    FIELDS
          No one ever proved that, but your
          new friend wrote in his novel that
          Burns was taking twenty thousand
          dollar bribes.

                    TRANBY
          Harris named Burns in the novel?

                    FIELDS
          Not exactly. He was real cleaver.
          He named the character Bur Nard
          Nathanson. Burns lost his job, his
          pension; eventually his wife and
          then he committed suicide. Thanks
          to Mr. Richardson.

Tranby's mouth falls open in shock.

                    TRANBY
          Wow, I'm sorry to hear that.

Fields tries to change the mood.

                    FIELDS
          By the way, when did he first show
          up?

                    TRANBY
               (enthusiastically)
          There you go. He showed up
               (expression changes)
          the day after the murderer's sketch
          appeared on the air.

                    FIELDS
          I want you to keep me posted.

                    TRANBY
          I'll be careful.

INT. YAMASHIRA MANSION - NIGHT

Takayama speaks to the council in the great room at the
Yamashira mansion.

                    TAKAYAMA
          That drawing is an exceptional
          likeness. His name is Martin
          Mayhew. We took control of his
          construction company, sold off the
          assets, and took the profit from
          him. He would have every reason to
          want to retaliate.

                    MRS. YAMASHIRA
          Was he Tanaka-Kai?

                    TAKAYAMA
          No, this is a farm boy. He grew up
          in some small town near
          Castroville, where his family
          raised artichokes. If he actually
          did this, he's working alone. We
          should just track him down and make
          him disappear.

                    OSUKA
          No one will miss him?

                    TAKAYAMA
          The police will give up on the
          investigation in due time.

                    OSUKA
          He has no family?

Takayama catches Osuka's drift.

                    TAKAYAMA
          No. His parents died when he was in
          his early twenties. He sold the
          farm and bought the construction
          company.

                    OSUKA
          No Aunts, Uncles, Siblings?

                    TAKAYAMA
          Not that I know of.

                    MRS. YAMASHIRA
          Why would the police give up on the
          investigation?

                    TAKAYAMA
          They just do, when they run into
          dead ends.

                    MRS. YAMASHIRA
          Why would I let them give up?

                    OSUKA
          What other options are there?

                    MRS. YAMASHIRA
          We should let the police find his
          body. That way they would think I
          have closure and we can move on in
          peace.

                    TAKAYAMA
          Too risky. No body, no evidence.
          No evidence, no crime.

                    OSUKA
          Good point. Where does he live?

                    TAKAYAMA
          Last I knew, he had a house in
          Oakland about the size of this
          room.

Everyone laughs at Takayama's joke. Until Mrs. Yamashira
speaks.

                    MRS. YAMASHIRA
          Do you think Tanaka-Kai hired him?

                    TAKAYAMA
          No Yamashira-sama. He has his own
          motives. I just didn't think he
          had the courage.

Tears well up in Mrs. Yamashira's eyes.

                    MRS. YAMASHIRA
          Do you think he kidnapped our son?

All the members of the council bow their heads in respect.

                    OSUKA
          We must find Mr. Mayhew and
          question him about Hiroshi.

                    TAKAYAMA
          I concur.

The Directors continue discussing a plan to get Martin.

INT. HARRIS' OFFICE - NIGHT

Harris types notes from the day's activities, peers out the
window and notices a conspicuous man across the street,
smoking a cigarette.

Harris picks up the phone and dials Tranby's number.

INTERCUT - HARRIS' OFFICE/TRANBY'S BEDROOM

                    TRANBY
          Hello.

                    HARRIS
          You Okay?

                    TRANBY
          Yes. They've assigned an officer to
          me, at least for the night.

                    HARRIS
          Me too.

                    TRANBY
          What do you mean?

                    HARRIS
          I mean I've been followed.

                    TRANBY
          Sorry.

                    HARRIS
          I'm certain you ought to find
          another place to stay until they
          catch this guy.

                    TRANBY
          Where would I go.

                    HARRIS
          Get a good night's sleep and I'll
          see you in the morning.

                    TRANBY
          Right. Like I'm going to be able
          to sleep until this guy is caught.

INT. HARRIS' LIVING ROOM - NIGHT

Harris approaches Susan as she watches the news. Melinda Gary
begins her report with Martin's sketch full on the screen.

                    MELINDA (V.O.)
          This man is still at large, and is
          still our top story. Tranby Croft,
          the artist of this sketch, was
          threatened tonight. Police believe
          the threats may have come from this
          man.

Harris grabs the remote and turns down the volume as he
reacts to the report.

                    HARRIS
          I can't believe that!

                    SUSAN
          Were you there?

                    HARRIS
          Yes and I can not understand how
          that story broke or why Tranby's
          own station would air it.

                    SUSAN
          Seems like they would want to keep
          it quiet. No wonder criminals keep
          terrorizing us, they get more
          publicity than Hollywood
          celebrities.

Harris paces around the room.

                    HARRIS
          How would you like to help me with
          this?

                    SUSAN
          In what way?

                    HARRIS
          Well, we ought to get Tranby out of
          her place and into another. I'm
          certain that I'll need your help
          convincing her to leave.

                    SUSAN
          She doesn't want to leave?

                    HARRIS
          Doesn't know where she'd go.

                    SUSAN
          What're you thinking?

                    HARRIS
          I don't know. We could invite her
          to dinner?

                    SUSAN
          Not here, let's go to a public
          place. I don't want that lunatic
          following her here.

                    HARRIS
          Good point.

INT. POLICE STATION - DETECTIVES PEN - SAME

Fields finds Ross asleep at his desk. He tries to awaken
Ross by walking close to the comatose detective. He coughs
lightly and clears his throat. He touches Ross lightly on
the shoulder. Nothing works. Frustration changes his
expression.

                    FIELDS
          Oh, for Christ's sake.

To which Ross jumps from his chair and stands at attention.

                    FIELDS
          At ease, detective. You okay?

                    ROSS
          Yes Sir!

                    FIELDS
          You a Peetnik?

Fields holds up two cups of Peet's coffee. Ross grabs one of
the coffees, which seems to calm him from the startled
awakening.

                    ROSS
          That would be great. Thanks, Dude.

                    FIELDS
          Ready to go on stake out?

                    ROSS
          Sure.

EXT. CHINA BASIN WAREHOUSE DISTRICT - NIGHT

Ross points to a warehouse with a sign which reads:

               "Bay Area Restaurant Supply"

                    ROSS
             This is it.

Ross and Fields enter a building directly across the street.

INT. STAKEOUT ROOM

Two cops dressed like plumbers salute Ross and Fields when
they step into the room. The surveillance equipment looks
very expensive. A large video camera points toward the supply
warehouse.

The BURLY PLUMBER motions for Ross and Fields to look at the
TV monitor which shows what the camera records as a figure
appears on the left side of the screen.

                    ROSS
             There's our guy.

The SLENDER PLUMBER moves the camera to follow Martin as he
approaches the building. Just as he gets to the door he
looks around. The camera operator zooms in to show a
flawless close-up of the man in Tranby Croft's composite.

                    FIELDS
             That's our boy. Good work, Men.

                    ROSS
             Let's go pick him up for
             questioning.

Fields nods and he and Ross salute the surveillance team and
leave the room.

EXT. CHINA BASIN WAREHOUSE DISTRICT

Fields and Ross walk in the street toward the Bay Area
Restaurant Supply building. About halfway across, the
building explodes. The two detectives soar up in the air and
then crash down on their backs. They scramble to avoid
flying debris.

                         ROSS
               Holy shit, Dude.

                         FIELDS
               Not funny, Ross.

MOMENTS LATER

The fire department arrives and puts out the flames, but the
building smolders pretty much gone. The DISTRICT CHIEF walks
over what's left of the warehouse and shrugs his shoulders at
Fields.

                         FIELDS
               Our man never came out?

Ross shakes his head.

                         DISTRICT CHIEF
               No bodies, just property damage.

                         FIELDS
               So he's still alive. Who owns,
               owned Bay Area Restaurant Supply?

                         ROSS
               Don't know yet, but I'll give you
               odds that it's the Yamashira
               Syndicate.

                         FIELDS
               First thing in the morning, See
               what John McGwire knows about this
               or what they're pursuing.

                         ROSS
               Happy to.

                         FIELDS
               I'll be on my way to Otafuku Tei to
               interview their manager, if you
               need me.

INT. OTAFUKU TEI RESTAURANT - DAY

Takayama stands at the Maitre 'D station. Fields hands
Takayama his card.

                         FIELDS
               Can we talk privately?

Takayama waves to a waiter, then leads Fields to a private
dinning area in the back of the restaurant.

PRIVATE DINING ROOM

Takayama motions for Fields to have a seat.

                    TAKAYAMA
          How may I help you detective?

                    FIELDS
          As you know, I'm investigating the
          murder of Mariko Yamashira. I hope
          I won't have to bother you too much
          during this ordeal.

                    TAKAYAMA
          He was my best friend, I'm happy to
          help.

                    FIELDS
          Best friend? How long had you
          known him?

                    TAKAYAMA
          Twenty-five... almost twenty-six
          years now.

                    FIELDS
          Do you know why he was here last
          Wednesday night?

                    TAKAYAMA
          To have dinner.

                    FIELDS
          By himself?

                    TAKAYAMA
          He and Mrs. Yamashira come here
          alone quite often.

                    FIELDS
          How often would you say?

                    TAKAYAMA
          At least once a week.

                    FIELDS
          Now on this occasion, you're quite
          sure that they had no intentions of
          meeting someone else?

                    TAKAYAMA
          They made reservations for two
          only.

                    FIELDS
          Would you mind if I looked at the
          reservation book?

                    TAKAYAMA
          Not at all.

Takayama walks away and returns with a ledger-sized book. He
flips it open to the page for the 4th of July, turns the book
towards Fields and places his finger on the entry where
Yamashira's name had been written.

Fields scans the rest of the page, finds nothing unusual.

                    FIELDS
          Thank you.

                    TAKAYAMA
          What troubles you Detective?

                    FIELDS
          If this was premeditated murder,
          then the killer had to know he
          would be here. I'm thinking he
          invited someone else.

Fields stares off into space, lost in thought.

                    FIELDS
          How did he know Yamashira would be
          out in the alley behind your
          restaurant? Doesn't make sense.

Takayama sits quietly. The two men stare at each other until
Fields breaks the silence.

                    FIELDS
          So, did Yamashira own this
          restaurant?

                    TAKAYAMA
          We share ownership. He was a
          silent partner, while I take care
          of the daily operations.

                    FIELDS
          Did he own Bay Area Restaurant
          Supply?

                    TAKAYAMA
          Yes.

                    FIELDS
          Were you partners in that
          enterprise as well?

                    TAKAYAMA
          Yes.

                    FIELDS
          What happened to it?

                    TAKAYAMA
          I believe one of our competitors is
          an arsonist.

                    FIELDS
          Why would they do that?

                    TAKAYAMA
          Because we are bigger and better at
          what we do, they feel they can
          strike a blow and take over our
          customers.

                    FIELDS
          Has that happened?

Takayama shrugs at the question.

                    TAKAYAMA
          It just happened last night.

Fields shows the composite to Takayama.

                    FIELDS
          Do you know this man?

                    TAKAYAMA
          No.

                    FIELDS
          Never seen him before?

                    TAKAYAMA
          Should I have?

                    FIELDS
          He was in the Bay Area Restaurant
          Supply last night when it exploded
          and an eye witness says he shot
          your best friend.

                    TAKAYAMA
          So, do _you_ know who he is?

                    FIELDS
          Not yet, but we will soon enough.

                    TAKAYAMA
          I'm sorry I can not help you,
          Detective.

Fields holds out the picture of Yamashira's insignia.

                    FIELDS
          Do you know what this is?

                    TAKAYAMA
          It is the mark of an outcast.

                    FIELDS
          Outcast?

                    TAKAYAMA
          He protested conventional wisdom in
          Japan. There was much in-fighting
          among the factions and as an anti-
          communist, he was a threat to the
          Japanese Government.

                    FIELDS
          What happened?

                    TAKAYAMA
          They actually placed him in Sugamo
          Prison, but he made a deal to be
          released. He promised to leave the
          country. The tattoo is a symbol of
          defiance.

                    FIELDS
          Right.

Fields' expression reveals a high bull shit index.

                    FIELDS
          So, he's actually a really great
          man, huh?

                    TAKAYAMA
          We call him the "Peace Maker."

                    FIELDS
          Peace Maker?

                    TAKAYAMA
          He worked very diligently to
          promote peace through out the
          factions.
                    (MORE)

                    TAKAYAMA (CONT'D)
          He preached non-violence and
          insisted that all his business
          associates behave according to the
          laws of the United States.

                    FIELDS
          Is that so?

                    TAKAYAMA
          Yes... Is there anything else you
          need at this time? I really must
          be getting back to my duties.

                    FIELDS
          That's it for now.

INT. NIKKO RESTAURANT - BAR - NIGHT

Harris and Susan sit at the bar having a drink. They talk and
laugh and appear to be having a good time.

Tranby glides into the restaurant. She looks very happy as if
anticipating a romantic evening alone with Harris.

She sees Harris and Susan at the bar. She adopts a sullen
look, crosses her arms over her chest. Harris looks up and
sees her at the Maitre 'D station. He gets up and approaches
her.

Tranby turns and begins to head for the door. Harris hurries
and catches her just before she reaches the door handle. He
grabs her arm and turns her toward him.

Harris looks at Tranby with disbelief.

                    HARRIS
          Where are you going?

                    TRANBY
          You've got a lot of nerve asking me
          here and then trying to pick up
          another woman.

                    HARRIS
          I wasn't trying --

                    TRANBY
          -- Oh, you cocky son of a bitch.

                    HARRIS
          Come here.

He pulls her toward the bar. She resists, but can't pull away
from his grip. They get to the bar where Susan sits. She has
seen the struggle. Tranby pulls away from Harris as they
reach the bar and tries to compose herself.

                    HARRIS
          Susan, I'd like you to meet Tranby
          Croft.

Susan holds out her hand to shake.

                    HARRIS
          Tranby this is my sister, Susan.

                    TRANBY
          Your sister? Oh my, I'm
          embarrassed.

                    SUSAN
          I'm flattered.

                    HARRIS
          I'm hungry.

INT. NIKKO RESTAURANT - TATAMI ROOM

Secluded behind shoji screens the threesome sits on the floor
at a traditional Japanese-style table. A kimono-clad
waitress slides back the screen and enters with a tray of
Maki rolls and other assorted sushi.

Harris picks up a Maki roll and takes a bite.

                    HARRIS
          Holy mackerel!

Tranby looks at him as if he's lost his mind.

                    HARRIS
          The chef here told me once that
          this was one of his specialties.
          It has mackerel and dried Bonita
          and a special sauce to cut the
          sharp flavor of the Bonita. He
          said if you like it you should
          holler "Holy Mackerel."

                    TRANBY
          Well that explains it, then.

A moment later the faint cry of "Holy Mackerel" comes from
some other place in the restaurant.

                    HARRIS
          See. You'll probably hear it
          often, for tonight it is especially
          tasty. Want a bite?

Tranby picks up a piece of tuna with her chop sticks.

                    TRANBY
          No thanks, I'll stick with the
          tuna.

The waitress backs out of the tatami room. Alone again,
Harris starts his pitch.

                    HARRIS
          Look, we think you should get out
          of your apartment. Lay low for
          awhile, until the killer is
          captured.

                    TRANBY
          I'm no good to society, if I'm
          hiding. Not working.

                    SUSAN
          What good are you to our community
          if you are killed? I mean even if
          you don't agree, wouldn't it be
          better to be safe than sorry?

Tranby looks at each of them back and forth.

                    TRANBY
          To tell you the truth, I have been
          thinking about it.

                    HARRIS
          Holy mackerel, Yes!

                    TRANBY
          Where am I going to go that would
          be safer than under Mitchell's
          protection?

                    SUSAN
          We've got a place for you, but we
          are concerned about being tailed.

                    TRANBY
          By whom?

                    SUSAN
          Well the killer for one.

                         HARRIS
               And the police. In order for you to
               be really safe no one should know
               where you are.

                         TRANBY
               You'll know.

She waits for his reaction. He makes a gesture with his
hands, shrugs his shoulders.

                         TRANBY
               I think we should tell Mitchell.

                         HARRIS
               Whatever you decide. But if you
               tell Mitchell, you run the risk of
               his disapproval or the police
               giving your position away. If you
               trust me not to tell, I think we
               should go without Mitchell's
               approval.

                         TRANBY
               I trust you, but I'm not convinced
               that this is the best move. On the
               other hand, I don't feel safe in my
               apartment anymore, especially with
               that dimwit Ross covering me.

The kimono-clad waitress enters the tatami again. She
carries their main course selections. She sets up a Seiro-
Mushi, which includes seafood, beef and vegetables.

While the pot heats up, she removes the appetizer dishes.
She places bowls of rice and other accompaniments at each
place setting. Then she begins stir frying their meal. She
puts on a real show. Once she serves the food, she takes the
cooking utensils and dirty dishes and backs out of the
tatami.

                         HARRIS
               Don't you just love this place?

The ladies smile a he's-such-a-guy kind of smile, almost
condescending in a female chauvinist way.

                         HARRIS
               What?

                         SUSAN
               Yeah, like you're clueless.

                    TRANBY
          Okay, I'll go with you, but if I
          feel the need I'm calling Mitchell.

                    HARRIS
          Fair enough. Give me the key to
          your apartment.

                    TRANBY
          What?

                    HARRIS
          We'll meet you there. Give us
          maybe a five minute head start.
          Then walk down Polk Street as if
          you are window shopping.

                    TRANBY
          I hope you know what you are doing?

                    HARRIS
          I write about it every day.

                    TRANBY
          That's fiction.

INT. NIKKO RESTAURANT - BAR

Harris and Susan see Ross at the bar with a clear view of the
front entrance. They look for another exit. Harris points
to a side door which leads to the lobby of the adjacent
hotel.

They hurry through the lobby and out to Van Ness Avenue.

EXT. VAN NESS AVENUE - NIGHT

Harris and Susan race down the street towards Tranby's
apartment.

INT. NIKKO RESTAURANT - BAR

Ross sees Tranby exit through the front door of the
restaurant and follows her.

EXT. POLK STREET - NIGHT

Ross follows Tranby as she walks down Polk Street, just as
Harris instructed. A large number of people crowd this
street, which gives Ross ample cover.

She stops in front of a shop and tries to see if anyone is
following her.

ROSS

turns away, so she cannot see him.

TRANBY

moves down the street. When she gets to Sacramento Street,
she turns the corner.

ROSS

hurries to the corner and peers around the hardware store
building, looking east.

TRANBY

crosses the street diagonally toward her apartment building.
She goes up the steps to the landing, disappears.

EXT. TRANBY'S BUILDING

Ross moves leisurely up the opposite side of the street,
lights a cigarette. He reaches in his coat and withdraws a
CHIC magazine. He puts one foot on the wall and leans back,
gets as comfortable as possible.

                    HENRY (O.S.)
          Evenin', Detective.

Ross jumps sideways as HENRY MILLS (35) exhales cigarette
smoke from his lungs. Henry in plain clothes looks like a
flatfoot right out of a film noir.

                    ROSS
          Man, you startled shit out a me,
          Henry! What's up?

                    HENRY
          Just thought you'd like to know,
          that Richardson fella' and a tall
          blonde went into that apartment
          building, maybe five minutes ago.

                    ROSS
          Thanks. Is there a back exit to
          this building?

                    HENRY
          Da'know. Maybe I'll go check it
          out.

                    ROSS
          If there is, stake it out.

                    HENRY
          Later, man.

TWENTY MINUTES LATER

Ross slips down the wall and crouches like a baseball
catcher.

TRANBY

wears a scarf as she exits the building. She carries a
Samsonite suitcase and matching make-up case.

ROSS

struggles to his feet and throws the cigarette butt away. As
he moves quickly up Sacramento street, he puts the magazine
in his coat. She gets too far ahead of him.

                    ROSS
          Excuse me, Miss Croft?

LARKIN STREET

She turns the corner and keeps walking. Now out of Ross'
sight.

He sprints to the corner to catch up.

Ross turns the corner and sees her about halfway up the
block. Ross runs faster. He catches her. He grabs her arm and
spins her toward him.

                    ROSS
          Miss Croft?

SUSAN

jumps away from him frightened.

                    SUSAN
          What do you want?

ROSS

shock on his face, has left his post for the wrong person.

                    ROSS
          Sorry Ma'am, I thought you were
          someone else.

EXT. TRANBY'S BUILDING

Tranby and Harris scurry down Sacramento Street in the
opposite direction from that taken by Susan. They quicken
their pace.

They turn the corner at the Polk Street end of the block out
of sight.

At the Larkin end of the block Ross turns the corner and
races to the stoop of Tranby's apartment building.

He runs up the steps, grabs the phone and presses 28. Then,
he slams the phone down; and, out of breath, rushes into the
street. He looks as if he has bungled another job.

EXT. CLAY STREET - NIGHT

On the north side of Clay Street, Harris and Tranby meet
Susan who is approaching from the opposite end of the block.
They get in his Firebird and the car pulls away.

EXT. GOLDEN GATE BRIDGE

Harris keeps the car's speed at the top of the limit, driving
north across the bridge.

EXT. SAUSALITO - NIGHT

The Firebird winds through the streets of Sausalito, turns
into an alley, and parks at the back door to DJ's Art Studio.

INT. WORKSHOP

DENNIS JOHNSON (35) a hippy, lost in the sixties, opens the
alley door as Harris, Susan, and Tranby approach.

                    HARRIS
          Hi Dennis.
               (to Tranby)
          Tranby, I'd like you to meet Dennis
          Johnson. He's an artist, although
          he sells others' art more than he
          sells his own.

                    DENNIS
          Don't believe a word he says,
          Tranby.

                    HARRIS
               (to Tranby)
          Dennis has offered his spare
          bedroom to you.

                    DENNIS
          Stay as long as you like.

Denis leads them into a workroom. Art tables and workbenches
fill the room with a variety of partially completed projects.

                    DENNIS
          This is the back of my shop.

An adjacent room contains framing equipment and supplies.
Dennis continues as he points to the framing room.

                    DENNIS
          It's really my workshop. I do the
          framing in there.

                    SUSAN
          Dennis is an art dealer with shops
          here in Sausalito and in Carmel.

                    DENNIS
          I'm opening another next month in
          Beverly Hills.

                    TRANBY
          On Rodeo Drive?

                    DENNIS
          Close, one block over. Beverly
          Drive. Well, look around. Make
          yourself comfortable. Do you have
          anything for me to take up to the
          loft?

                    HARRIS
          No not really. Dennis, I really
          appreciate this.

                    DENNIS
          No problem.

INT. DENNIS' LOFT - NIGHT

A bed, small dresser, some other small furniture, nothing
fancy, the way a man would decorate. As Harris enters the
room, Tranby looks out a large picture window toward San
Francisco Bay. Harris approaches her from behind.

                    HARRIS
          Quite a view isn't it?

                    TRANBY
          Indeed.

The City lights, bright across the Bay, reflect in the water,
as does the moonlight. At about 8:00 p.m., Harris massages
her shoulders.

                    HARRIS
          A penny for your thoughts?

                    TRANBY
          Just contemplating the day.

                    HARRIS
          Are you frightened by all this?

                    TRANBY
          Just wondering how long I'm going
          to be a fugitive?

                    HARRIS
          Hopefully not long.

She turns to face him.

                    TRANBY
          Are you involved in this in anyway?

                    HARRIS
          I'm not sure I get your meaning.

                    TRANBY
          Harris, I think I'm falling in love
          with you and I need to know, _now_,
          why you happened to show up just at
          the time --

                    HARRIS
          -- Wait a minute, you're not
          suggesting I could be connected
          with the murderer. Are you?

                    TRANBY
          Well it does seem pretty
          coincidental that I wasn't having
          this trouble until you showed up.

                    HARRIS
          I'm trying to protect you.

                    TRANBY
          So are the police, but I'm not with
          them. I chose you!

                    HARRIS
          That's a laugh! The police... um...
          the police don't protect people.
          They can't even do anything until
          something happens to you. Victims
          don't have civil rights, but there
          sure are a lot of criminals out
          there on those streets, because
          some cop didn't read 'em their
          rights properly, or --

                    TRANBY
          -- Harris, I need to know.

He takes her face in his hands and looks straight into her
eyes.

                    HARRIS
          I'm a good guy... white hat... John
          Wayne type. Howdy Ma'am.

Tranby smiles. Harris kisses her passionately.

                    HARRIS
          You get some rest, I'll check in
          tomorrow.

                    TRANBY
          You're leaving?

                    HARRIS
          Thought I'd go see what's happening
          at your place.

                    TRANBY
          Don't go.

                    HARRIS
          You think I'm going to rendezvous
          with my murderous partner and let
          him know you're out of the picture.

She kisses him passionately.

                    TRANBY
          Stay!

Harris walks out of the loft and leans over the stair case.

                    HARRIS
                 (yells)
          Susan.

Susan appears at the bottom of the stairs.

                    HARRIS
          Will you ask Dennis to take you
          home? Leave my car and I'll be home
          later.

Susan says nothing. She merely winks approval.

HARRIS

goes back into the bedroom and closes the door.

TRANBY

smiles seductively and bites her lower lip.

HARRIS

embraces and kisses her passionately.

SERIES OF SHOTS - TRANBY AND HARRIS MAKE LOVE

A) She unbuttons his shirt.

B) He removes her clothes in a controlled, sensual way.

C) He admires her breasts and touches the erect nipples.

D) She pushes him playfully. He tumbles to the sheets.

E) She unbuckles his pants and pulls them off.

F) She crawls on top, straddles him.

G) He rolls her over and assumes the top position.

H) Their tempo quickens and as they climax the sound of
something like, "Take my breath away," by Berlin can be
heard.

BACK TO SCENE

Harris rolls off of her. They breathe heavily and appear worn
out.

                    HARRIS
          I had no idea.

They cuddle together.

INSERT - CLOCK, WHICH READS:

          "11:00 P.M."

BACK TO SCENE

Harris gets out of bed and dresses. Tranby awakens.

                    TRANBY
          What's wrong?

                    HARRIS
          Nothing, but I still want to go see
          what's happening at your place.

                    TRANBY
          Don't leave now.

                    HARRIS
          I'll be back in two hours at the
          latest. I promise.

                    TRANBY
          I'll hold you to it.

He leans over and kisses her goodbye.

                    HARRIS
          Rest up for round two.

                    TRANBY
          You're on!

EXT. TRANBY'S APARTMENT BUILDING - NIGHT

Martin and Aaron drive past the front of the building in a
pale blue Chevy, heading west on Sacramento Street. Police
cars double park in front of the building. Fields and Ross
talk to one another near the stoop.

INT. MARTIN'S CAR

The two criminals discuss the matter.

                    MARTIN
          This place is crawling with cops.
          Let's get outta here.

                    AARON
          Wonder what's goin' on?

EXT. SACRAMENTO STREET

Harris' Firebird turns the corner, nose points at the Chevy.

Martin looks straight at Harris.

Harris recognizes Martin.

Aaron slams down the accelerator. The Chevy jumps out ahead
of The Firebird. The chase is on, as Harris hits his
accelerator.

The Chevy makes the turn onto Van Ness, skidding across two
lanes of traffic. He nearly clips oncoming cars. The Firebird
follows close behind.

Both cars weave in and out of traffic on Van Ness. Aaron
turns right on Broadway, Harris follows.

Aaron goes left at Hyde Street with Harris on his tail. Aaron
turns right on Lombard Street and begins his descent down the
crookedest street in the world. The car smashes into walls
that protect the homeowners flowers and walkways. Harris
follows, but gets a little further behind.

Aaron turns right on Leavenworth and right again on Greenwich
Street before Harris finishes his descent down Lombard.
Harris turns right on Leavenworth.

INT. HARRIS' CAR

From inside The Firebird the streets ahead appear empty.

                    HARRIS (O.S.)
          Fuck!

EXT. LEAVENWORTH

The Firebird moves south on Leavenworth, but a little bit
slower as if he were coasting. As Harris crosses Greenwich,
he looks west and sees The Chevy at the next intersection.
Harris puts it in reverse and then in forward and makes the
turn. He accelerates as quickly as he can.

Aaron turns left on Larkin Street and left again going east
on Filbert Street. Harris gets close enough to see the
second turn.

The Chevy climbs Filbert. Harris follows.

They're very close to Hyde Street.

                    HARRIS
          Turn, you son of a bitch.

Aaron continues up Filbert crossing Hyde.

> HARRIS
> Damn you!

Just past Hyde Street, Filbert, drops at about a forty five degree angle toward Leavenworth. Aaron takes the jump at fifty miles per hour.

Harris speeds toward the jump point. The Chevy sails through the air.

About 100 feet down from the pinnacle, The Chevy smashes to the pavement.

Harris slams on the brakes.

> HARRIS
> Damn it!

The Firebird goes into a slide and comes to a stop.

The right tires of The Firebird perch precariously on the edge of the cliff.

EXT. HARRIS' CAR

He jumps from the driver's side out into the street and runs to the back of the car.

Looking east on Filbert, Harris sees The Chevy turn left on Jones street heading toward Fisherman's Wharf.

EXT. TRANBY'S BUILDING - NIGHT

Fields strolls toward his car. Harris pulls up next to one of the patrol cars. He jumps out of the car.

> HARRIS
> (to Ross)
> Hey, I just saw the guy whose
> picture was on BayTips.

Ross approaches Harris.

> ROSS
> Where?

They stand near the front end of The Firebird.

> HARRIS
> He was headed toward the
> Wharf.
> (MORE)

                    HARRIS (CONT'D)
          He's driving a pale blue Chevy...
          probably late 60's, maybe a '68 or
          '69 Impala.

                    ROSS
              (takes out a note pad)
          Did you get the license tag number?

                    HARRIS
          Yes. California plates, 1 NYN 750.

                    ROSS
          Thanks. Can you hold on for a
          minute?

Ross yells to stop Fields

                    ROSS
           Mitchell! Mitchell! <u>Dude</u>!

Ross waves to get Fields to return.

FIELDS

Just as Mitchell Fields pulls on the door handle of his car,
he looks up to see Ross waving. He wears a puzzled
expression. Fields lets go of the door handle and walks
toward Ross and Harris.

ROSS

speaks to Harris

                    ROSS
          Thank you Mr. Richardson. I'd like
          you to talk to Detective Fields,
          he's in charge of this
          investigation.

Fields arrives.

                    ROSS
              (to Fields)
          He just saw the suspect.

                    FIELDS
          Richardson, what have you done with
          Ms. Croft?

                    HARRIS
          Did I miss something? He just told
          you I've seen your murderer. In
          fact, I've been chasing the son of
          a bitch all over San Francisco.

                    FIELDS
          I appreciate your interest in this
          case, Mr. Richardson, but I can't
          protect Ms. Croft from a murderer,
          if I don't know where she is.

                    HARRIS
          I don't know where she is.

                    FIELDS
          I think you do.

Two alpha males face-to-face.

                    HARRIS
          Well you're wrong, but even if I
          did know, I wouldn't tell you.

                    FIELDS
          Mr. Richardson, would you come with
          me?

                    HARRIS
          You dumb ass. I've just told you I
          saw the murderer and you don't go
          after him, you don't even call it
          in. All you want to do is harass
          me. What the hell is the matter
          with you?

                    FIELDS
          I'll tell you what the matter is, I
          think you have something to do with
          this. And I'm going to prove it.
                    (in Harris' face)
          You get me, Mister?

                    HARRIS
          Yeah, I get you. You're just plain
          stupid.

                    FIELDS
          That's enough of the insults,
          Mister.
                    (to Ross)
          Ross, I'd like you to arrest Mr.
          Richardson, read him his rights and
          escort him downtown, and I'd like
          for you to interrogate Mr.
          Richardson until you find out --
                    (to Harris)
          -- where the Fuck Tranby Croft is.
                    (to Ross)
          Is that clear?

                    ROSS
          Yes, Sir.

                    HARRIS
          What's the charge?

                    FIELDS
          Well, obstruction of justice for
          starters. I'll think of some other
          things to add to the report before
          the night's over.

                    HARRIS
          Are you going to at least go look
          for the murderer?

                    FIELDS
          Yeah.
               (to Ross)
          Get him outta here.

Ross takes Harris to a patrol car, handcuffs him and puts him
in the car.

FIELDS

At the same time, approaches McNally.

                    FIELDS
               (to McNally)
          Call this in. We got the suspect
          spotted in a blue Chevy.

INT. POLICE STATION - NIGHT

Ross ushers Harris to the printing area.

INSERT - INK PAD

Ross presses Harris' fingers into the ink and places them on
the rap sheet.

HARRIS

stands in front of a camera, holds a placard with his name,
date, and prisoner number. Ross shoots two mug shots.

INT. INTERROGATION ROOM

Ross and Harris face each other at a table. Ross talks to
Harris and Harris shakes his head. Ross gets nothing.

Fields enters the room. They continue talking. Fields loses his temper. He grabs Harris by the collar and picks him up. Fields smashes Harris into the wall.

                    HARRIS
          You'll be lucky to keep your badge
          the way this is going.

                    FIELDS
          Fuck you.

                    HARRIS
          I'm not talking to you without
          advice of counsel, and Ross here
          hasn't let me make that phone call
          yet.

Fields drops Harris.

                    FIELDS
               (to Ross)
          Let him make the call and then
          throw his ass in the holding tank.

PUBLIC WALL TELEPHONE

Harris whispers as to not be overheard.

INTERCUT - HARRIS' WALL PHONE/SUSAN'S APARTMENT PHONE

                    HARRIS
          Susan, I've been arrested.

                    SUSAN
          For what?

                    HARRIS
          Obstruction of justice.

                    SUSAN
          Where are you now?

                    HARRIS
          I'm at SFPD headquarters. Listen,
          you've got to do two things.

                    SUSAN
          Of course, what?

                    HARRIS
          Call Watson and see if he can get a
          writ of habeas corpus to get me out
          of here. Then, move Tranby to
          Carmel.

                    SUSAN
          Why move her?

                    HARRIS
          I just think she'll be safer.

                    SUSAN
          Okay, if you say so.

                    HARRIS
          And you better call her now. I told
          her I'd be back tonight. She'll be
          worried when I don't show.

                    SUSAN
          No problem. Anything else?

                    HARRIS
          No thanks. I'll see you in the
          morning.

FIELDS' OFFICE

Ross enters as Fields fills out paperwork at his desk.

                    ROSS
          He just called someone and told
          them to move her to Carmel.

                    FIELDS
          Who did he call?

                    ROSS
          It was his home phone. Somebody
          named Susan, answered.

                    FIELDS
          Thanks.

INT. YAMASHIRA MANSION - DAY

Mariku Yamashira lays on a special bed in the great room.
His feet point south toward San Francisco. A formal white
kimono covers his body, with the bottom-portion up by his
head. His most prized Samurai sword lays on top of the gown.
Circling the bed, Japanese folding-screens rise, upside down.

Mrs. Yamashira sits next to her husband. Incense burns next
to a bowl of rice, the makura-meshi. A lone chopstick adorns
the center of the bowl. She prays to Buddha.

Osuka approaches Mrs. Yamashira. He touches her shoulder.

                    OSUKA
          The people from the mortuary are
          here.

                    MRS. YAMASHIRA
          Show them in.

The people from the mortuary wheel a casket into the Great
Room. They place Mr. Yamashira's body into the casket. They
place the kimono and the sword on his body as it was for the
wake.

Then they add some paper money, a headband with a triangle in
the center, some cigarettes, and candy. They close the
casket and wheel it out to the hearse.

INT. BUDDHIST TEMPLE - DAY

Thousands of people squeeze together. Fields shoves his way
through the crowd.

The casket sits in front of the alter. The PRIEST picks up a
wooden tablet and places it on the alter in front of the
casket.

Fields leans toward a YOUNG JAPANESE MAN next to him.

                    FIELDS
          Do you speak English?

                    YOUNG JAPANESE MAN
          Quite well actually.

                    FIELDS
          Is this Mariku Yamashira's funeral?

                    YOUNG JAPANESE MAN
          Yes.

                    FIELDS
          What is the Priest doing now?

                    YOUNG JAPANESE MAN
          He is inscribing the kaimyo...
          posthumous name.

                    FIELDS
          Posthumous name?

                    YOUNG JAPANESE MAN
          Like an honorary name. It helps
          prevent the spirit from coming back
          when his earthly name is called.

                        FIELDS
            What is Yamashira's posthumous
            name?

                   YOUNG JAPANESE MAN
            Loosely translated it means
            "Compassionate Godfather."

MONTAGE - THE FUNERAL RITUAL

-- The Priest reads the Sutra.

-- Mrs. Yamashira starts a procession to the casket. She
clasps her hands in prayer, bows, and tosses incense into an
urn. When the fresh incense hits the smoldering embers in
the urn, it hisses and a puff of smoke rises from the urn.
She clasps her hands together, prays, bows, and returns to
her seat.

-- Osuka, Takayama, and the other Directors follow the same
procedure in hierarchical order.

-- The Priest chants and finishes the Sutra.

-- Osuka, Takayama, and four other Directors hoist the casket
and march it outside the temple to the hearse.

-- The pallbearers unload the casket at the crematorium and
deliver it to the metal rack which allows the casket to slide
right up to the cremation chamber door.

-- The attendant hands Mrs. Yamashira a key, which she in
turn hands to Osuka.

-- The family leaves to have the funeral banquet.

-- They return to the crematorium later, where the attendant
gives the urn to Osuka and hands a set of chopsticks to each
family member.

-- Osuka unlocks the chamber door and slides the casket out.
The attendant opens it.

-- Family members position themselves around the casket. They
pick bones out of the ashes and place them into the urn with
the chopsticks.

-- The attendant points to the Adam's apple. Osuka and
Takayama move quickly to the location and share the honor of
moving the most important piece to the urn.

-- When the urn is full, the attendant places the lid on top,
wraps it with a white cloth, and hands it to Mrs. Yamashira.
She, again, hands it to Osuka for safekeeping.

EXT. BAY BRIDGE - DAY

Fields, Ross, and McNally drive an unmarked car across the
Bay Bridge toward Oakland.

FREEWAY EXIT

The car turns off, goes into a neighborhood, and disappears
from sight.

CAR

It slows and stops in front of a row of stucco house that all
look alike. The three detectives get out of the car and
proceed up the street.

MARTIN'S HOUSE

They march until they are in front of a house two doors up
from the car.

                    FIELDS
          McNally, get around back. Ross,
          cover the other side. I'll try to
          get him to come to the door.

The two detectives hustle to their posts. Fields stops.

As Fields pans the neighborhood, there is no activity.

REAR OF HOUSE

McNally sneaks past the windows and positions himself at the
right rear corner of the house. He waves at Fields to let him
know he's in position.

ROSS

gives the OK signal.

FIELDS

takes a deep breath and approaches the front door.

MARTIN'S FRONT DOOR

Fields knocks on the door. No answer. He rings the door bell.
No answer.

                    FIELDS
          Anybody home?

                    SALLY (O.S.)
          Looking for Mr. Mayhew?

Fields spins, puts his hand on his revolver and looks toward
the street.

MARTIN'S FRONT YARD

SALLY LIPPITT (30) heavy-set, stands on the sidewalk with her
hands on her hips. She wears a flowered housedress, a large
yellow hat with a purple scarf tied around the band, and pink
Converse tennis shoes.

                    FIELDS (O.S.)
          Yes, I am.

                    SALLY
          Hasn't been here since the fourth
          of July.

                    FIELDS
          You sure?

                    SALLY
          Absolutely.

Fields approaches the woman. Ross comes out from the side of
the house.

                    FIELDS
               (to Ross)
          Get McNally.
               (to Sally)
          I'm Detective Mitchell Fields,
          SFPD.

He flashes his shield.

                    SALLY
          I've been expecting you since I saw
          Martin's picture on BayTips.

                    FIELDS
          Are you the one who called BayTips?

                    SALLY
          Yes.

                    FIELDS
          What's your name?

                    SALLY
          Sally Lippitt.

                    FIELDS
          Ms. Lippitt, how do you know he's
          not been here since the fourth?

                    SALLY
          I been watchin' the house. He's
          been acting peculiar.

                    FIELDS
          In what way?

                    SALLY
          Leavin' at all hours. That kinda
          thing.

                    FIELDS
          Nothing to call the Police about, I
          guess?

Ross and McNally join the conversation, as Sally begins her
answer.

                    SALLY
          Look Detective, as far as I know,
          Mr. Mayhew is an upstanding
          citizen. He owns his own
          construction company. He's a
          member of my church. He does
          community service and, although
          I've never been in his house, I've
          heard that he has a picture of
          himself with the President for good
          grass roots work with the
          Republican party... Now you tell
          me, does that sound like the
          profile of a murderer?

                    FIELDS
          No ma'am it certainly doesn't.
          Unfortunately, we have an
          eyewitness that says he killed
          somebody... So, what made you call?

                    SALLY
          When he ran.

                    FIELDS
          Ran?

                    SALLY
          After the first BayTips report, I
          started watching the house to see
          what his reaction would be.

                    ROSS
          What was that?

                    SALLY
          Nothing. He went to work, came
          home, just like a normal day.

                    MCNALLY
          Then?

                    SALLY
          Then, after the second BayTips, I
          saw him load his car with a
          suitcase and drive away. He hasn't
          been back since.

                    FIELDS
          Maybe he just went on a business
          trip?

                    SALLY
          Maybe, but then I started worrying
          about the screams.

                    MCNALLY
          What screams?

                    SALLY
          I'd been awakened by what I thought
          were screams... but in the fog here
          it's hard to tell where they were
          coming from. They were faint. I
          wasn't even sure if they were real
          or if I was just dreaming.

                    ROSS
          What did they sound like?

                    SALLY
          Like a young boy crying out. I
          figured it was some kid on drugs.
          You know, a bad trip.

                    FIELDS
          Why didn't you call the police?

                    SALLY
          I did. They sent a patrol car out
          the next day. The officer
          interviewed people on our block and
          left. He called me and told me it
          must have been a cat fight.
               (a bit miffed)
          That was no cat fight!
                    (MORE)

                    SALLY (CONT'D)
For God's sake, I know what a cat
scream sounds like and that was no
cat!

                    MCNALLY
That must have been a very
disappointing result for you.

                    FIELDS
Do you have any idea where Mr.
Mayhew may have gone?

                    ROSS
Was he alone?

                    SALLY
He drove away alone, but there was
another man.

                    ROSS
Can you identify this other man?

                    SALLY
No, but I know what his car looks
like.

                    MCNALLY
What kind of car?

                    SALLY
Light blue Chevy, kind of big --
not like the compacts that they
make now a days.

                    MCNALLY
License number?

                    SALLY
Couldn't see it, but the plate was
black -- Doesn't that mean its
twenty-five years old?

                    FIELDS
Could be. Anything else you can
tell us?

                    SALLY
That's about it.

                    FIELDS
Thank you. You've been very
helpful.

Fields hands her his card.

                    FIELDS
          If he comes back, would you call me
          directly instead of BayTips?

The three detectives head back to the car.

                    FIELDS
          (to the other detectives)
          I want to get a search warrant.

                    MCNALLY
          Let's just go in now.

                    FIELDS
          We can't go in until we have a
          search warrant.

                    MCNALLY
          That could take forever.

                    FIELDS
          Martin Mayhew must be considered
          innocent until proven guilty.

                    ROSS
          I think we've got probable cause.

                    MCNALLY
          Come on. I can get us in, we'll do
          a quick run through, if it's clean,
          we'll leave, no harm done... If
          not, we'll get the search warrant.

                    FIELDS
          No!

They get to the car and get in.

INT. CAR

The conversation continues.

                    MCNALLY
          Come on, Boss.

                    FIELDS
          I don't want you guys to blow this
          bust.

                    MCNALLY
          Okay, you go get the warrant and
          we'll go on stake-out... If he
          comes back, we'll make sure he
          doesn't destroy any evidence.

                    FIELDS
          Right! And as soon as I'm out of
          sight, you two assholes break in
          and blow the case.

                    MCNALLY
          Okay, I'll go get the warrant and
          you two stay.

                    FIELDS
          All right.

EXT. STREET

Ross and Fields get out of the car and check their equipment,
weapons, radios, etc.

McNally slides into the driver's seat, drives away.

Fields and Ross approach Sally Lippitt's house.

CAR

McNally turns the corner and then another corner. Then he
stops the car, gets out, and starts walking through a yard.
McNally hops a fence.

FIELDS AND ROSS

They get to Sally's driveway.

                    ROSS
          I'll go camp out in the back yard.

                    FIELDS
          Okay, I'll let you know if he comes
          back.

ROSS

Ross crosses the street.

FIELDS

Fields goes to Sally's front door. He knocks and she answers.

                    FIELDS
          Ma'am, we've decided to stake out
          this house for awhile. Would you
          mind if I used your living room?

                    SALLY
          I guess not... come on in.

She opens the door. He steps in.

                    SALLY
          Can I get you some coffee?

                    FIELDS
          Please.

ROSS

rounds the back corner of the Mayhew house.

McNally is at the back door picking the lock. McNally jumps
and draws his weapon.

                    MCNALLY
          You scared the shit out of me, man.

ROSS

rushes to McNally, who is now back to work on the lock.

                    ROSS
          What are you doing?

                    MCNALLY
          What does it look like I'm doing?

                    ROSS
          Don't do it. You're going to be in
          deep shit.

                    MCNALLY
          Where's Fields?

                    ROSS
          Across the street.

MARTIN'S BACK DOOR

The door swings open. McNally stands and pushes the door as
if to let Ross enter first.

                    MCNALLY
          Come on, we can do this faster with
          two.

                    ROSS
          I don't know, man.

McNally enters the house.

Ross stammers and stutters, obviously having a mental
jousting match about whether to enter or not. After a moment
he goes in.

INT. MARTIN'S HOUSE - DAY

McNally enters the bedroom.

                    MCNALLY
          Ross, come here.

As Ross enters the bedroom, McNally puts on surgical gloves.
McNally picks up a pair of handcuffs.

                    ROSS
          What do you think this guy's been
          up to?

                    MCNALLY
          I shutter to think.

                    ROSS
          What's that smell?

McNally ignores the question. Puts the handcuffs down and
walks to the closet. He opens the closet door.

CLOSET SHELVES

overflow with sweaters, belts, and other items. On one shelf,
slightly above the detective's eye level, rest half a dozen
wallets. McNally reaches up and brushes his hand over the
first few inches of the shelf. He hits one of the wallets and
it falls.

McNally's other hand snatches it from midair. He opens it.
He reads the ID.

                    MCNALLY
          Uh oh!

                    ROSS
          What now?

                    MCNALLY
          Remember the Yamashira family had a
          son?

                    ROSS
          Insisted that he'd been kidnapped?

                    MCNALLY
          Yeah. This is the boy's wallet.

Ross goes to the closet and pulls down the other wallets and
they fall to the floor. Ross squats down. Rapidly, he opens
each wallet, looks at the ID, and then tosses it aside. When
done, he looks up at McNally.

> ROSS
> (rather melancholy)
> The two boys from the oil drums and
> the rest are the other Japanese
> people from the missing persons
> file. We've got enough. You better
> go get the search warrant.

Both detectives double time from the bedroom into the hall.
About halfway down the hall Ross stops.

> ROSS
> What's that smell, Dude?

> MCNALLY
> I don't know. Smells a little like
> sewage.

> ROSS
> Sweet though. I've smelled it
> before.

> MCNALLY
> Who ever heard of sweet sewage?

> ROSS
> Oh, no! It's the morgue. I've
> smelled this odor at the morgue.

The two detectives sniff the air, trying to locate the origin
of the putrid smell.

> ROSS
> Let's go. When you get back with
> the search warrant, we'll find the
> source.

EXT. MARTIN'S HOUSE

The two detectives exit the back door. McNally starts for the
corner of the yard, while Ross heads in the other direction.
McNally stops and looks at the side of the house.

> MCNALLY
> Ross!

Ross runs toward McNally. McNally points to a door, which may
lead to a basement.

                    MCNALLY
          Let's go in here for a second.

                     ROSS
          I'd rather not.

McNally opens the door.

                    MCNALLY
          Jesus H. Christ.

Both men gag from the stench. McNally pulls his coat up over
his face.

INT. BASEMENT

As the detective walks through an inch of water.

A very dark basement, the only light comes from the open
door. Ross sees some hair on a workbench.

McNally approaches the bench. McNally reaches into his coat
and pulls a plastic bag, picks up the hair and puts it in the
bag. At that moment, a cat jumps from the darkness. The cat
lets out a hideous screech as he hits Ross near the head, and
then leaps toward the door. The cat lands in the water and
jumps quickly out the door to safety.

Ross and McNally laugh a very nervous laugh.

                     ROSS
          Thank God. Let's get outta here.

                    MCNALLY
          Just a minute.

McNally takes a flashlight from his belt.

He shines the light on the back wall of the basement. It
appears to be made of dirt. He shines the light on the
workbench until he finds a spade.

He takes the spade and splashes his way to the back wall.

                    MCNALLY
          Ross, hold this light for me.

McNally tosses the flashlight to Ross.

THE DIRT WALL

McNally takes a shovel full of dirt, and another. Then, he
pulls the shovel from the wall a third time and it contains a
clot of decomposing flesh. It's white and soapy looking,
almost like soft lard.

McNally goes for another scoop of earth, but hits something
hard. He takes the spade and pries it into the earth.

A skull pops out of the soft earth.

McNally pulls away from the wall of earth.

> ROSS
> Holy shit. Now will you get out of
> here and get the warrant?

EXT. MARTIN'S HOUSE

McNally and Ross come out of the basement.

Detective Fields stands in front of his two men.

Looks of surprise, like little boys who have been caught
stealing candy by a merchant.

> FIELDS
> You'd better have a good fucking
> explanation for this.

> MCNALLY
> It's my fault, Sir. I talked Ross
> into it.

> FIELDS
> (to McNally)
> Oh, I know that. What I don't know
> is what I'm going to do with your
> ass when the court throws this case
> out because of your illegal search.

> MCNALLY
> Yes, Sir. May I go get the search
> warrant now? We believe this place
> is full of missing persons.

> FIELDS
> Full of missing persons?

> ROSS
> Missing Japanese persons, Sir.

                    FIELDS
          And what makes you feel that way?

                    ROSS
          We saw wallets in the master
          bedroom, and a skeleton --

                    FIELDS
          -- You've been in the house too. Oh
          this is just fucking great.

Fields paces, rubs his face.

                    FIELDS
          Okay, here is what we are going to
          do. We are all going to go get the
          warrant, because I'm not letting
          you two idiots out of my sight.

                    MCNALLY
          What about the stake out?

                    FIELDS
          We'll call a patrolman to sit in
          front of the house. Now where is
          the car?

                    MCNALLY
          Next street over.

                    FIELDS
          Ross, go get it.

Ross trots toward the back fence, McNally and Fields head for
the front of the house.

INT. OTAFUKU TEI RESTAURANT - NIGHT

The funeral party sits in a large private dinning area. All
heads turn toward a loud knock at the front door. Takayama
motions for everyone to continue, as he leaves to see who is
knocking.

FRONT DOOR

Takayama pulls back the curtain to disclose Detective Fields.

                    TAKAYAMA
          We're closed!

                    FIELDS
          I need to talk to Mrs. Yamashira.

                    TAKAYAMA
          She's in mourning, Detective.

                    FIELDS
          I have news about her son.

                    TAKAYAMA
          Wait here.

Takayama rushes back to the dinning table and whispers in
Mrs. Yamashira's ear. She nods, rises slowly, and Takayama
escorts her to the front of the restaurant. He unlocks the
door and holds it open for Fields to enter.

                    FIELDS
          I'm sorry to bother you, Mrs.
          Yamashira, especially on this day.
          I'm afraid I have some bad news to
          share and a request.

                    MRS. YAMASHIRA
          What could be important enough to
          interrupt our funeral customs?

                    FIELDS
          My detectives found evidence that
          may prove the man who shot your
          husband also murdered your son.

Mrs. Yamashira's knees buckle. Takayama catches her and
helps her to a chair, where she sits with her head between
her legs.

Takayama sits next to her, rubs her back. Fields stands on
the other side.

Finally, she raises her head.

                    MRS. YAMASHIRA
          I'm sorry. Was there something
          else?

Fields rubs the back of his neck. He doesn't want to do
this.

                    FIELDS
          Yes, I'm sorry about this. We can't
          identify him from his driver's
          license photo.

A dreadful sound comes from somewhere deep inside her.

                    TAKAYAMA
          Do you have to do this now,
          Detective?

                    FIELDS
          The sooner the better, I'm afraid.

                    TAKAYAMA
          Well get on with it.

                    FIELDS
          We need something to confirm DNA...
          toothbrush, hair sample, dental
          records.

Mrs. Yamashira passes out.

                    TAKAYAMA
          I'm sure we can get those things
          for you, just not this minute.
          They would be back at the house in
          Tiburon anyway.

                    FIELDS
          How soon?

                    TAKAYAMA
          Tomorrow?

                    FIELDS
          How about tonight after you have
          finished your duties.

                    TAKAYAMA
          Meet me there at ten.

Fields turns to leave. As he reaches the front door, he
turns back toward Mrs. Yamashira. She has lifted her head,
but appears groggy.

                    FIELDS
          I'm sorry for your loss.

He leaves the restaurant before anyone can respond.

INT. CARMEL STUDIO - DAY

Tranby and Susan sit in the studio office when Harris enters.
The two women stand and approach him.

                    TRANBY
          Are you all right?

                    HARRIS
          Yes, but I did have a scare.

                    SUSAN
          What happened?

                    HARRIS
          The murderer was following me to
          Dennis' studio...

The women look panicked.

                    HARRIS
          ...don't worry I lost them.

                    SUSAN
          Are you sure?

                    HARRIS
          Yes, I'm sure!

                    TRANBY
          That does it. I'm going to take
          control.

                    HARRIS
          What do you mean?

                    TRANBY
          I'm tired of being the victim here.
          I am going to be hiding until this
          guy is arrested; so, I'm going to
          do something to get him arrested.

                    HARRIS
          Don't be foolish now.

Harris paces around the office.

                    TRANBY
          Look Harris, I can't live like
          this.

                    HARRIS
          Susan, tell her to listen to
          reason.

                    SUSAN
          Tranby, maybe you should tell the
          police where you are, like you
          wanted to before.

                    HARRIS
          That wasn't what I had in mind.

                    SUSAN
          Harris, you are a writer of
          fictitious murders. This could get
          you killed. You've already been
          chased by a man whom we believe is
          a serial killer. I don't
          particularly like the idea of him
          getting any closer to any of us.

                    TRANBY
          So forget the idea of your trying
          to protect me. I'm calling Mitch.

Tranby goes to the phone. She dials.

                    TRANBY
          Yes, would you please connect me
          with the San Francisco Police. This
          is an Emergency!

INT. POLICE STATION - DAY

Oskie answers the phone.

                    OSKIE
          San Francisco Police Department.

                    TRANBY
          I need to speak to Detective
          Fields, please.

                    OSKIE
          Who's speaking?

                    TRANBY
          This is Tranby Croft.

                    OSKIE
          Miss Croft, Detective Fields is at
          the television station trying to
          locate you. Where are you?

                    TRANBY
          I'm at Dennis Johnson's Art Studio
          in Carmel. I want you to tell
          Detective Fields that I want to
          help... Never mind, I'll call the
          station.

At the dial tone, Oskie hangs up the phone.

INT. CHRIS WILLIAMS' OFFICE - DAY

Chris Williams, Fields, McNally, and Ross are in her office.

                    CHRIS
          I haven't heard from her in quite
          some time.

                    FIELDS
          It's important that we find her
          before the murderer does. We
          believe that he is responsible for
          all the Japanese who have
          disappeared --

                    CHRIS
          -- You think I'm withholding from
          you detective? If I knew anything,
          I'd let you help her.

                    ROSS
          When was the last time you heard
          from her?

                    CHRIS
          I don't really remember. It must
          have been about the time of the,
          um, report we did about the break
          in.

INT. T.V. STUDIO

Melinda Gary strolls past the crew and toward Chris Williams'
office. As she gets to the desk just outside the office door,
the phone rings. Melinda looks around to see where the
secretary is. Locating no one, she picks up the receiver.

                    MELINDA
          Chris Williams' office.

                    TRANBY
          Chris?

                    MELINDA
          This is Melinda Gary.

                    TRANBY
          Melinda, Tranby, is Chris there?

                    MELINDA
          She's in a meeting.

                    TRANBY
          With Mitchell Fields?

                    MELINDA
          Hold on.

Melinda walks to and opens the office door.

                    MELINDA
              (to Chris)
          Do you want to take any calls?

                    CHRIS
          No. Would you mind taking a
          message?

                    MELINDA
          Not at all.

Melinda walks back to the phone.

                    MELINDA
          She asked me to get all the
          details. Where are you?

                    TRANBY
          That seems strange. Did you tell
          them it was me?

                    MELINDA
          Of course. Where are you?

                    TRANBY
          I'm in Carmel. Listen, I want you
          to do something for me.

                    MELINDA
          Of course, where are you in Carmel?
          Shall I give Chris your phone
          number?

                    TRANBY
          No that won't be necessary. Um,
          I've got a plan to get the guy who
          is murdering all those people. I'll
          be sending you some drawings
          tonight so leave me some time. In
          fact, don't plan anything for
          tonight's show.

                    MELINDA
          Okay, but how can I get in touch
          with you?

                    TRANBY
          I'll call you later. Be at the
          studio at three this afternoon

Tranby hangs up the phone.

INT. DJ'S PLACE

Tranby approaches Harris and Susan.

>   TRANBY
>   That was strange. I asked Melinda
>   to tell Chris and Mitch I was on
>   the phone and she said they told
>   her to take a message.

>   SUSAN
>   Melinda is hiding something.

>   HARRIS
>   What?

>   TRANBY
>   I don't know, yet. But we've got to
>   find out. <u>You've</u> got to find out.
>   You're the one that got me into
>   this mess.

>   HARRIS
>   I did?

>   TRANBY
>   Yes. I should have stayed at my
>   place.

>   HARRIS
>   You're better off here.

>   SUSAN
>   How is she better off here? How are
>   any of us better off here?

>   HARRIS
>   Look, I know you are both upset
>   with me, but trust me they can't
>   find you here.

>   TRANBY
>   I don't like this. I feel like a
>   sitting duck just waiting.

>   HARRIS
>   Okay, what do you want me to do?

>   TRANBY
>   Think! Why the hell is Melinda
>   behaving like this? I want you to
>   take some drawings to her then
>   follow her.

                    HARRIS
          I don't want to leave you here.
          I'll have Susan take them.
          Melinda's never seen her.

                    TRANBY
          She could pose as a delivery
          person... That's good... Let me
          draw.

INT. AARON'S HOUSE - DAY

Martin talks with an unseen person.

                    MARTIN
          I don't know where she is.

                    MELINDA (O.S.)
          Carmel can't be that big.

Melinda Gary stands before Martin.

                    MARTIN
          You don't have any more information
          for me than Carmel.

She shrugs.

                    MELINDA
          Tranby is going to send me some
          drawings to the studio, when they
          arrive I'll call you on the mobile
          phone. Now, get your little butt
          headed in that direction. I'm going
          to go back to the studio.

INT. T.V. STUDIO - DAY

Melinda Gary sits in Chris Williams' office. Susan approaches
with a package. She wears blue jeans and a Giants' baseball
cap. She looks like the stereotypical delivery kid that rides
a bike around San Francisco. She chews bubble gum.

Susan blows a bubble and after it pops...

                    SUSAN
          Anybody here named Melinda Gary?

Melinda stands and drifts toward Susan.

                    MELINDA
          I'm Ms. Gary.

                    SUSAN
          Delivery from Tranby Croft.

Melinda takes the package and begins opening it immediately.

                    MELINDA
          Thank you.

Melinda turns and heads away.

                    SUSAN
          What, no tip?

                    MELINDA
          Bill me.

Susan flips her off. Melinda scurries around the corner.

Melinda has the drawings open. One is of Martin standing
over a body. Melinda Gary is in the background of the drawing
as if she is witnessing the murder.

Melinda changes to the second drawing which is a full face of
Martin and a full face of Melinda side by side.

Melinda rushes to a pay phone at a remote end of the
corridor. She dials.

                    MELINDA
          Martin, Tranby is on to us. She
          wants me to air a drawing of you
          and me together. Yes, and get
          this, she even wrote the copy,
          listen, "Melinda Gary host of
          BayTips is Murderer's Accomplice.
          Anyone knowing the whereabouts of
          either of these people should call
          B A Y - T I P S." I don't know
          what she's up to but I do know
          where she is.

Melinda looks closely at the delivery slip.

                    MELINDA
          It's called "DJ's Place." It's an
          art studio on Lincoln Street. 432
          Lincoln Street.

SUSAN

Susan stands around a corner listening to the conversation.
As Melinda hangs up the phone, Susan runs softly out of
sight.

EXT. BATTERY STREET - DAY

Harris and Susan talk on the street.

> SUSAN
> She's involved all right. She just
> called a guy named Martin and told
> him where Tranby is, just like we
> thought.

> HARRIS
> Good!

TV STATION DOORS

Melinda dashes out of the building toward the parking garage.

INT. PARKING GARAGE

Melinda hurries through the garage when Harris jumps out from
behind a pillar and grabs her by the arm. He shoves the gun
in her ribs.

> HARRIS
> Don't make a peep or I'll blow you
> away.

Melinda is frightened, but doesn't say a word.

> HARRIS
> We're going to walk out to the
> street nice and calm and get into a
> car. Do you understand?

Melinda nods.

EXT. CALIFORNIA STREET

Harris puts the gun hand inside his coat and with the other,
escorts Melinda to the car. Susan in the driver's seat.
Harris opens the back door and pushes Melinda into the back
seat. The car drives away.

EXT. CARMEL - DAY

The blue Chevy slowly pulls into town.

INSERT - SIGN, it reads:

> "Welcome to Carmel"

BACK TO SCENE

The car cruises down Ocean Avenue.

INSERT - SIGN, it reads:

        "Carmel Art Association"

An arrow on the sign points right.

EXT. DOLORES STREET

The blue Chevy turns onto Dolores Street and pulls into a
parking place on the street. Martin and Aaron get out of the
car. They stroll to the building entrance.

INT. CARMEL ART ASSOCIATION

Martin and Aaron enter the office. A very attractive female
CLERK greets them.

                    MARTIN
          We want to tour some of the art
          galleries. Don't you have a list of
          some of the preferred studios?

The clerk gets a brochure.

                    AARON
          I've heard of a studio called DJ's
          Place. Where is that?

                    CLERK
          It's on Lincoln Street. Not far...
          Here is a map of the village...
          See.

Martin and Aaron take the map.

                    AARON
          Thanks a lot.

EXT. DOLORES STREET

They jump into the car and head for DJ's Place.

EXT. DJ'S PLACE

They get out of the car and walk to the studio entrance.

INT. DJ'S PLACE - FOYER

A small, well stocked art studio. Paintings, sculptures, and other art pieces are all around. A nice looking RECEPTIONIST (25) sits at a desk near the entrance.

                    RECEPTIONIST
          Welcome to DJ's Place. Looking for
          anything in particular?

                    MARTIN
          Yes, actually.

Aaron goes past the receptionist and looks around the studio.

                    RECEPTIONIST
          I'll be happy to point out any
          particular artist's work. We have
          many contributors.

Aaron returns.

                    AARON
          Looks empty to me.

Aaron goes to the front door, tosses the "CLOSED" sign on the glass and locks the door.

                    RECEPTIONIST
          What's... going on?

                    MARTIN
          Anybody else here?

                    RECEPTIONIST
          Why... yes, as a matter of fact.

                    MARTIN
          Why don't we go get them?

Martin grabs the girl and escorts her to the back of the studio.

INT. DJ'S PLACE - WAREHOUSE

When the threesome get to the back part of the building, it also appears empty.

                    MARTIN
          Anybody home?

No response.

                    RECEPTIONIST
                  (Screams)
              Fire! Fire!

She breaks away from Martin and starts running. Aaron throws
a shoulder block into her and bumps her to the ground.

                    AARON
              I don't think anyone can hear you,
              miss.

                    MARTIN
              Now tell us where Tranby Croft is.

                    RECEPTIONIST
              Who is Tranby Croft?

                    MARTIN
              That's not the right answer. If you
              tell us, we won't hurt you.

Tears run down the receptionists cheek.

                    RECEPTIONIST
              I really don't know. I've been on
              vacation... came back a day early.
              I don't know what you're talking
              about.

Martin bends down and picks the girl up from the floor. He
takes a gun from his vest holster and places it between her
legs. He runs the cold steel up her thigh, lifting her skirt
up to the crotch.

THE GIRLS HIPS

The gun barrel rubs against her panties.

                    MARTIN (O.S.)
              Does this feel good?

She's barely able to get it out through the sobs.

                    RECEPTIONIST (O.S.)
              No.

Martin pushes her up against an art table. She falls back and
lays at a 45 degree angle. Martin pulls the gun from between
her legs and steps closer. He pushes his pelvis hard against
her pubic bone.

                    MARTIN
              Does this feel better?

The receptionist is frozen in terror. Martin grabs her face
with his left hand squeezes her mouth open and inserts the
gun barrel.

                    MARTIN
          I can't hear you!

Martin moves his face in closer.

                    MARTIN
          You've got about 30 seconds to tell
          me where Tranby Croft is or I'll
          blow your head clean off.

                    AARON
          You better tell him, honey. He's
          not a very nice man.

The receptionist nods her head and Martin removes the gun.

                    MARTIN
          That's more like it.

                    RECEPTIONIST
          They may be in Sausalito.

                    MARTIN
          Where in Sausalito?

                    RECEPTIONIST
          The other studio Dennis has there.

                    MARTIN
          Address?

The gun comes up toward her head.

                    RECEPTIONIST
          It's on the brochure.

Aaron grabs a brochure and reads it.

                    AARON
          Got it.

Martin moves away from the girl.

He starts to walk away. Turns and fires a shot that hits the
girl in the chest. Blood spatters over the table as the girl
slumps to the floor and dies.

                    MARTIN
          Thank you.

EXT. DJ'S PLACE - SAUSALITO STUDIO - DAY

Harris drives up to Dennis' place. Susan, Harris and Melinda
get out of the Firebird and Harris ushers Melinda into the
studio.

INT. DJ'S PLACE - SAUSALITO STUDIO

Tranby watches Harris shove Melinda into a chair.

          TRANBY
What's going on, Melinda?

          MELINDA
That's what I want to know. Why
have you kidnapped me?

          HARRIS
More like a citizen's arrest.

          TRANBY
You're trying to have me killed and
I want to know why?

          MELINDA
What in the world makes you think
I'm trying to have you killed?

          SUSAN
Don't be coy.

          TRANBY
Let's review the facts, shall we? I
turn in a picture of a suspected
felon and you tell the world I'm
the artist. That's against BayTips
policy.

          HARRIS
Not to mention down right stupid.
And then you announce that she's
being threatened by the murderer,
on the air.

          SUSAN
That seems rather strange to us.
But when I overheard you just call
the guy on the phone and tell him
where she was, now that was too
much for us to overlook.

          MELINDA
Circumstantial evidence counselors.

                    TRANBY
          Melinda, spill it.

                    MELINDA
          Or what?

Harris walks over to Melinda and slaps her off the chair.

                    HARRIS
               (yells)
          Or we beat the shit out of you.

                    MELINDA
          I'll sue your ass off for this.

                    HARRIS
          If you don't start talking, you
          won't be able to.

Harris picks Melinda up and chucks her back into the chair.
Susan marches over to Melinda and pushes Harris away.

                    SUSAN
          You're going to tell us what we
          want to know, one way or another.
          What'll it be?

                    MELINDA
          I can't help you get Martin.

                    TRANBY
          Why? What's your connection?

                    MELINDA
          I can't help you, Tranby.

Harris smacks her again.

                    MELINDA
               (yells)
          You cut that out.

                    HARRIS
          You don't seem to understand who's
          holding the cards here.

                    SUSAN
          One way or another, hmm?

                    TRANBY
          Tell us, or we'll call Mitchell.

There is a long pause as Melinda thinks through her strategy.

                    MELINDA
          So, if I tell you, you won't call
          Mitchell?

                    TRANBY
          Right.

Another pause as Melinda thinks.

                    MELINDA
          You'll let me go?

                    TRANBY
          Depends on what you tell us.

                    MELINDA
          Okay, I'll take a chance that
          you'll understand...
               (searches their eyes for
                commitment)
          Martin is my brother.

                    SUSAN
          Your brother?

                    TRANBY
          Why is he killing these people?

                    MELINDA
          They forced him out of business.
          These Japanese are taking over the
          world. They bought Pebble Beach
          for Christ's sake.

                    TRANBY
          You don't kill people, because they
          are buying and selling companies.

                    MELINDA
          Martin worked his whole life to
          build that business. He buys
          American. He can't believe no one
          is stopping them from buying our
          entire country. And quite frankly
          I find it distasteful to think that
          they --

                    HARRIS
          -- Oh shut up.

                    TRANBY
          How long have you known?

                    MELINDA
          Only since you drew his composite.
          I tried to get him to stop, but he
          is like an insane maniac over this.
          Yet, he's still my brother and I
          don't want to lose him.

                    TRANBY
               (to the group)
          Should we call Mitch?

                    HARRIS
          Yes, call him.

                    MELINDA
          You said if I told you, you
          wouldn't call the police.

Tranby picks up the phone and dials.

INTERCUT PHONE CONVERSATION - TRANBY'S STUDIO/MITCHELL'S
OFFICE

                    TRANBY
          Mitchell Fields? Tranby Croft
          calling.

The others watch in silence as the operator puts the call
through.

                    FIELDS
          Tranby, where the hell are you?

                    TRANBY
          I'm at DJ's Place in Sausalito. How
          soon can you get here?

                    FIELDS
          I'm on my way! Maybe 30 minutes.

                    TRANBY
          Hurry Mitch. Martin may be on his
          way too!

                    FIELDS
          What do you mean?

                    TRANBY
          I made contact with him. We've got
          Melinda Gary.

                    FIELDS
          Melinda Gary?

                    TRANBY
          She's involved. She's made contact
          with Martin and told him enough to
          be able to find us.

                    FIELDS
          Jesus Christ, Tranby.

                    TRANBY
          Don't lecture me Mitch, just get
          here.

Tranby hangs up the phone.

EXT. GOLDEN GATE BRIDGE - DAY

The blue Chevy crosses the bridge.

EXT. POLICE STATION - DAY

Mitchell, McNally, and Ross hurry into their car. Two other
pairs of officers get into two marked cars. The three cars
pull away fast. The unmarked vehicle is in the lead.

EXT. DJ'S PLACE - SAUSALITO STUDIO

The blue Chevy drives past the front of DJ's Place and slowly
pulls into a parking space. Martin and Aaron get out of the
car.

                    MARTIN
          You go around back.

Martin continues alone toward the front of the studio. He
enters.

INT. DJ'S PLACE - SAUSALITO STUDIO

The front lobby is set-up much like the Carmel showroom. No
one is around. Martin puts the "CLOSED" sign on the front
door and locks it.

EXT. DJ'S PLACE - SAUSALITO STUDIO

At the rear entrance, Aaron approaches the workshop door. He
looks around for witnesses, sees none and pulls his gun. He
enters the building with gun raised.

INT. WORKSHOP

Aaron creeps in. The others see Aaron with his gun out and
scatter to various parts of the workshop.

Harris dives behind one of the workbenches and tips it over as a shield.

Tranby runs into the framing room.

Harris sticks his head up, over an art table.

Aaron makes a break for the framing room.

Harris pulls his gun and fires at Aaron to protect Tranby. He misses.

FRONT LOBBY

Susan crashes through the door between the workshop and the lobby. Martin grabs her and puts his gun to her head.

> MARTIN
> Perhaps you should tell me what's
> going on in there!

FRAMING ROOM

Tranby hides behind a large cabinet that houses mat board stock.

Aaron pushes through the doorway, eyes like a rabbit's darting around, he checks the environment. He moves slowly through the room.

WORKSHOP

Harris runs to the entrance of the framing room. He listens at the door for a moment. He pushes the door open.

Aaron spins and fires at the movement of the door.

Harris jumps back against the wall just outside the framing room door.

Aaron moves around the room looking for Tranby. He gets closer to the cabinet where she hides.

Tranby looks around her location for something, anything that might be used as a weapon. She spies a mat cutting knife.

INSERT - KNIFE

Tranby picks up a knife like the one she uses at the TV Station.

Aaron turns the corner, where Tranby was. She's not there.

Tranby comes up from behind Aaron and slashes his neck with the mat cutting knife.

Aaron spins toward her at point blank range and points the gun at her. Tranby swings the knife at the gun and hits Aaron in the wrist with the blade. The gun discharges, and falls to the floor.

Tranby and Aaron dive for the gun. They scuffle as they both try to get it. The gun fires again.

WORKSHOP

Harris pushes the door again. No shot is fired, so he sneaks into the framing room.

LOBBY

Martin pushes Susan through the door into the workshop. He holds her in front of his body as a shield.

EXT. DJ'S PLACE - SAUSALITO STUDIO

Mitchell and the other police officers arrive with lights flashing. They jump out of their respective cars Mitchell waves at the team as if to say, "encircle the place."

INT. WORKSHOP

Martin moves through the workshop with Susan. No movement in the studio.

Melinda sticks her head up from behind a pile of boxes, like a mouse.

Martin spins and points his .45 in Melinda's direction.

                    MARTIN
          Where are they?

Melinda points to the framing room door.

Martin slowly moves to the framing room, still using Susan as a shield. He pushes her forward into the room.

As soon as Martin is out of site, Melinda runs to the Lobby door.

LOBBY

Melinda races through the Lobby, unlocks the front door and charges outside.

EXT. DJ'S PLACE - SAUSALITO STUDIO

Mitchell catches Melinda as she tumbles from the studio.

                    FIELDS
          What the hell's going on in there?

                    MELINDA
          Martin's got a girl and he's going
          after the others.

                    FIELDS
          Where?

                    MELINDA
          In back through the workshop.

INT. FRAMING ROOM

Martin and Susan stand in the middle of the framing room.

Tranby and Harris squat behind a cabinet. Aaron lays dead on
the floor.

                    MARTIN
          You have put me in a very awkward
          position. I'm sure you understand
          that I have no choice but to kill
          you all.

                    HARRIS
          We understand completely.

Tranby throws the mat cutting knife at Martin.

He ducks out of reflex, but loses his grip on Susan. She
breaks away. Martin spins and fires.

The bullet hits her in the shoulder. Probably not a mortal
wound, but a really solid hit in the shoulder blade. It
throws her to the floor. She scrambles behind a workbench.

Martin fires again, but misses.

Harris shoots Martin in the arm.

In the commotion, Tranby moves to get a better angle. She
shoots Martin in the chest with Aaron's gun.

Wounded severely, Martin turns and runs quickly through the
door.

A gun discharges. Martin staggers backward through the door
and falls face up at Tranby's feet.

Mitchell walks through the door, cautiously.

All eyes are on Martin. He still breathes. Mitchell kneels down to Martin's face. Blood pours from a wound in his neck.

                    MARTIN
          Takayama paid me to make the hit.

Martin dies.

Ross and McNally await their orders.

                    FIELDS
          I'm going to go tell Mrs. Yamashira
          that Takayama sanctioned the hit.
          Ross, take our beloved news anchor
          to the station and book her for
          accessory to murder.

                    ROSS
          Yes, Sir...
               (as he rambles off)
          Okay, Dudette.

                    FIELDS
          McNally, go arrest Takayama.

                    MCNALLY
          My pleasure, Boss.

The two detectives leave. Fields turns to Tranby.

                    FIELDS
          You going to be all right?

                    TRANBY
          Yeah... sooner or later.

                    FIELDS
          I'll send EMS to check your
          vitals... and you need to come in
          tomorrow to make your statements,
          OK?

                    TRANBY
          Yes, Sir.

INT. TRANBY'S APARTMENT - STUDIO - DAY

Tranby bends over the art table within her apartment
developing some drawings for the BayTips show. The intercom
buzzes.

SUPER: "SIX MONTHS LATER"

She straightens up and starts for the door. Stops. Adds just
a little more color to the sketch. Hesitates. Then proceeds
to the door constantly looks back at the drawing until she
leaves the room.

HALLWAY - FRONT DOOR

She lifts the telephone handset.

EXT. TRANBY'S BUILDING

Harris Richardson stands at the front door holding a handset
to his ear. Tranby's voice comes through the speaker.

>   TRANBY (O.S.)
>   Who is it?

>   HARRIS
>   Harris Richardson.

>   TRANBY (O.S.)
>   What do you want?

>   HARRIS
>   I'm a writer and I'd like to talk
>   to you.

HALLWAY - FRONT DOOR

Tranby smiles a very seductive smile.

>   TRANBY
>   Come up to the third floor. It's
>   Suite 208.

She pushes the buzzer.

INT. TRANBY'S APARTMENT - STUDIO

Tranby goes back to the drawing table and continues working
on her sketch.

Harris enters the studio carrying a package. He walks over to
the drawing table and grimaces when he sees the drawing of a
faceless man standing behind a woman. The man holds a large
knife. The woman, her throat cut, screams in terror. It is
very graphic.

>   HARRIS
>   That is gruesome!

                    TRANBY
          She's alive.

                    HARRIS
          You've got to be kidding?

                    TRANBY
          No, I'm not. I've got an interview
          with her today.

                    HARRIS
          Wow.

                    TRANBY
          Yes, and she can't talk.

                    HARRIS
          How are you going to get her to
          give you a description of the guy,
          if she can't talk?

She holds up her sketch pad and a handful of Prismapastel
Pencils.

                    TRANBY
          I have this and a professional
          assortment of Prisma colors.

                    HARRIS
          Well, I'll be interested to hear
          how it turns out.

He hands her the package.

                    TRANBY
          I love presents!

She tears into the wrapping and out pops a book.

INSERT - BOOK COVER, it reads:

                    "The Tranby Croft Affair"

The cover shows an artist drawing a crime scene.

BACK TO TRANBY

Tranby admires the book.

                    TRANBY
          This is great. I hope it sells
          well.

                    HARRIS
          I think it will. Thanks for your
          help on this one.

                    TRANBY
          You're welcome.

                    HARRIS
          You want to work on another with
          me?

Tranby looks at him, bewildered.

                              FADE OUT.

Bibliography

BIBLIOGRAPHY

Ackerman, Angela & Puglisi, Becca *The Emotion Thesaurus: A Writer's Guide to Character Expression* (Self-Published, 2012).

Brooks, Larry *Story Engineering* (Cincinnati: Writer's Digest Books, 2011).

Egri, Lajos *The Art of Dramatic Writing* (New York: Touchstone Books, 1960).

Field, Syd *Screenplay* (New York: Dell Publishing, 1982).

Goldman, William *Adventures in the Screen Trade* (New York: Warner Books, 1983).

Goodman, Linda *Love Signs* (New York: Harper Perennial, 1992).

Goodman, Linda *Sun Signs* (New York: Bantam Books, 1971).

Hauge, Michael *Selling Your Story in 60 Seconds* (Studio City: Michael Wiese Productions, 2006).

Keirsey, David *Please Understand Me II: Temperament, Character, Intelligence* (Del Mar, CA: Prometheus Nemesis Book Company, 1998).

King, Viki *How to Write A Movie in 21 Days* (New York: Harper Collins, 1988).

Kosberg, Robert *How to Sell Your Idea to Hollywood* (New York: HarperPerennial, 1991).

Maass, Donald *The Fire in Fiction* (Cincinnati: Writer's Digest Books, 2009).

McKee, Robert *Story* (New York: ReganBooks, 1997).

Seger, Linda *Advanced Screenwriting* (Los Angeles: Silman-James Press, 2003).

Seger, Linda *Making a Good Script Great* (Hollywood: Samuel French Trade, 1994).

Simon, Neil *Rewrites* (New York: Simon & Schuster, 1996).

Snyder, Blake *Save the Cat!* (Studio City: Michael Wiese Productions, 2005).

Snyder, Blake *Save the Cat! Strikes Back* (Saline: McNaughton & Gunn, Inc., 2009).

Trottier, David *Dr. Format Tells All* (Cedar Hills, UT: Applewood Arts, 2012).

Trottier, David *The Screenwriter's Bible* (Los Angeles: Silman-James Press, 2005).

MOVIE QUOTES
(from page 59)

"You had me at 'Hello.'"   -- *Jerry Maguire*

"You can't handle the truth."   -- *A Few Good Men*

"There's no crying in baseball."   -- *A League of Their Own*

"I'll be back."   -- *The Terminator*

"I'll have what she's having."   -- *When Harry Met Sally*

"Go ahead, make my day."   -- *Sudden Impact*

"I ate his liver with some fava beans and a nice Chianti."
                                            -- *The Silence of the Lambs*

"Toto, I have a feeling we're not in Kansas anymore."
                                            -- *The Wizard of Oz*

"You're gonna need a bigger boat."   -- *Jaws*

"I'm not bad, I'm just drawn that way."   -- *Who Framed Roger Rabbit*

www.ingramcontent.com/pod-product-compliance
Lightning Source LLC
Chambersburg PA
CBHW061750250726
48657CB00001B/61